rest(less)

Enter Your
Personal & Professional
Promised Land

rick sbrocca

Dedication

This book is dedicated to you –
living fully alive all of the time.

Figure 1

Table of Contents

Alpha   vii

Part One *The Parable of the Restless Prodigal*   1
  The Restless Son   3
  The Responsible Brother   23
  The Rest Giving Father   37

Part Two *Personal Promised Land Playbook*   51
  Forty Years or Forty Days?   53
  Purpose   59
    The 7Rs of Rest   63
  Priorities   89
    The 7Fs of Freedom   91
  Time   107
  Goals   115
  Action   119

Part Three *Professional Promised Land Playbook*   125
  Culture: The Margin of Victory   127
    The 7Vs of Victory   137

Omega   171

Acknowledgements   177

Blessing   179

Endnotes   182

Alpha

What's In This Book For You

Welcome to the starting line. You are about to begin the race of your life: the race *for* your life. The reward? A life fully lived!

That is an immense promise, but the inspired words you hold in your hands *will* change your life. *Restless* is a compass that provides directions to "true life north." You *can* flourish through all trials and triumphs. How? Through a proactive and sustainable breakthrough to your personal and professional victory.

We are all restless in one way another. We struggle with our life purpose — knowing it, implementing it, or both. When you admit to that struggle, you find yourself ready to transform your restlessness into restful productivity. By rest, I mean being at ease while being excellent in every area of your life. Restlessness turns to restfulness.

As we begin, let's enter into a mutually beneficial transaction right now. My role/responsibility is that of a messenger bringing a gift to you. I am like the UPS driver delivering a package of powerful tools to your front door. A gift, however, cannot open itself. Your role/responsibility is to open your heart while opening your gift. The next step is to test the contents of the gift, put them to work, and win.

Who am I to think I have something to offer you? Like you, I am a quality-of-life student who has conducted plenty of experiments. (I have also had plenty of experience blowing up the lab, and I would like to help you avoid my mistakes.) I am not a motivational speaker, life coach, theologian, scholar, preacher, or evangelist. I am simply a lifelong seeker of the true meaning of an abundant life. I have tasted extreme failure and extreme success. I know I am not perfect; however, I am certain that an all-consuming fire rages in my heart to see you avoid life's pitfalls and fully experience abundant life victory.

So, how close to victory are you? On your abundant life victory gauge, where does the needle fall between empty and full?

Figure 2

Okay, enough of living a less than full life; it is time to fill it up. I have successfully tested these life lessons on hundreds of individuals and in a large variety of workplace cultures. Additionally, I have invested countless hours developing simple and practical processes to teach sustainable life improvement. These life lessons will help you to simplify the explosion of information, complexity, and rapid pace in our world today. *Restless* is an interactive resource designed for an excellent user experience.

I am a kinesthetic learner, so this learning curve is based upon heart, action, and perseverance. No theory here, just traction. You will win this race by accelerating your learning curve. We will focus on optimizing your purpose, priorities, time, health, relationships, money, and work. Your accelerated growth will deliver new life victory, saving you precious resources.

Figure 3

Live Different

This is not a self-help book. I have experimented with all the self-help stuff. Something about the "self" part did not work for me. This book is not a religious book. I have also experimented with religion. Something about the "manmade" part failed to work for me. Supernatural results require supernatural power. My present and everlasting help comes directly from above. *Restless* is a joint venture between Holy Spirit power and proven, practical, and sustainable best practices. I have discovered an *unconditional, love-driven,* life success multiplier for my friends and coworkers. Do not worry if you do not believe in my power source: you will still benefit, and you can form your own conclusions. All are welcome, and all are honored.

This book is also a label-free zone. I have successfully worked with friends labeled as Jewish, Muslim, Buddhist, Evangelical Christian, Catholic, Mormon, Agnostic and Atheist. I have taught in environments as diverse as Fortune 500 companies, Inc. 500 companies, venture-backed start-ups, small business turnarounds, churches, universities and municipal governments. As one people, we share the common denominator of seeking significance in life; we want to be fully loved and to love fully. *Restless* is the training ground for a new generation of life innovators who are ready to risk going the distance for life/work victory.

Race to win, but race with joy and expectation. *Restless* is not here to save you from a near-death experience; it is here to save you from a near-life experience. It is not here to raise the dead but to raise the living into abundant life.

An Overview of

Restless

Part One
The Parable of the Restless Prodigal

This is a contemporary version of the parable of the prodigal son. Based on a true story, this tale is about looking for love and success in all the wrong places. What happens when you have climbed the mountain of success and realize that you are on the wrong mountain? The good news is that you can start fresh at any point in life. The better news is that you can begin to implement viable, heart-led, step-by-step plans. The best news is that you can reach a new place in your life that is better than you have ever imagined.

Part Two
Personal Promised Land Playbook

Get ready to enter your *Personal Promised Land*. To do so, you will complete a comprehensive and detailed review of where you are now and what barriers you need to conquer in order to advance. Purpose empowers personal and professional victory. You will be introduced to a customizable purpose-finding process of revelation, relative, relationship, responsibility, results, renewal, and rewards. You will also move through a personalized *Life Ecosystem* for freedom in faith, fitness (spirit/mind/body), family, future (work), finances, friends, and fun. You will receive real-world, proven and practical tools for your personalized goals, plans, and actions. This process requires a burning desire for a better life and the discipline to follow through for your victory.

Part Three
Professional Promised Land Playbook

Now you are ready to enter your *Professional Promised Land*. This landscape is designed to optimize your work victory through voice, vision, values, value-added, validators, vortex, and velocity. Here, you also discover innovative ways to lead work culture for the betterment of the workers, the community, and the overall success of the work venture.

Both the *Personal Promised Land* and the *Professional Promised Land* sections are enhanced by interactive tools that are available at RestlessTheBook.com. Make the most of all of the *Restless* resources and enter your promised lands.

Let's Go!

We are the CEO's of our lives. We are ultimately responsible for our own life leadership. Life leadership is having the humility to examine ourselves and improve what we find. Life leadership requires boldness to confront and change the status quo to reach our fullest destinies. *Restless* is not about creating fans or followers; it is about creating empowered life leaders. It is not a book for everyone, but then again, you are not everyone. Before we turn on the new, let's turn off the old, namely the old paradigm of a limited life. Say "Goodbye" to a scarcity mentality and "Hello" to an abundance mentality.

As you read, let your open heart and spirit absorb the material first and then filter it to your mind. You will be creating an environment where personalized and optimized communication rhythm will flourish. Declare this statement out loud: "I open my spirit, heart, and mind to live a life changed for the better." It does not matter if the initial change is small or large, only that you are advancing. *Restless* is engineered to bless and sustain those who are passionate about living fully alive, all of the time. Your time-is-now hourglass has just turned upside down. The abundance of the moment is now flowing in your favor.

Ladies and Gentlemen, let the race begin; your race for abundant life victory starts today...

PART ONE

The Parable
of the Restless Prodigal

The Restless Son

R E S T L E S S. The word scrolled across the giant LED of Gabriel's imagination as he walked through Times Square. He did not notice the digital billboards advertising flat screen televisions and Swiss watches, though he could afford anything flashing on those screens.

On the brink of forty, Gabriel looked like he had it all. With his Italian heritage, well-cut suit, and classic overcoat, he could have been mistaken for a New York City mob boss on his way to dinner. Yet earlier that day, at his investment banker's office on Fifth Avenue, Gabriel had closed the biggest deal of his life. A deal that equaled a seven-digit payday for his family.

"Seven digits!" he thought to himself. How could the word "restless," which had driven him his entire life, still rattle him, let alone grow louder? He had already been successful by most people's standards, and now his long-sought business triumph was finally complete: a Fortune 50 firm had just bought his start-up company, *Voice Innovation International,* which held the intellectual property for a cutting-edge invention. This new technology seamlessly

controlled all smart phone functions through extremely accurate voice recognition across fourteen languages.

After a sixteen-year journey, Gabriel had achieved one of his largest dreams. He seemed to have everything else figured out, too. His good health, happy family, and community life convinced him that he had reached the pinnacle of life success; today should have been the final proof of that success. In the investment banker's office, Gabriel had signed his name to the contract and sat back in his chair. Michael, his close friend and business partner, had wept with joy. Gabriel had just smiled, but something had not felt right.

Actually, he could not feel anything, and he wondered where his emotions were. *I should feel happier than this,* Gabriel thought. Even his heart felt frozen, unable to sense the wealth of celebration. *Is this what I've been sacrificing for?* Work had been his all-consuming passion and the reason for missing so many family nights, children's games, and friends' special occasions. *This* was the payoff. *This* was the remarkable event that was supposed to bring complete joy and happiness to his life. *Where is the feeling of having finished? Of being fulfilled?*

Ever since Gabriel could remember, his restless nature had driven what he called a life search, a deep longing to fulfill his destiny. To him, his life search was the ultimate search engine for discovering the meaning and purpose of life. Gabriel thought that the acquisition process would be it. But was it? Surely the current peak experience was a large part of the life search that had begun when he was a boy.

Gabriel found himself standing still beneath the bright diodes of a super screen's ad for an investment company. A model family in designer clothing was laughing while walking along an exotic coastline. The screen stretched up several stories, almost big enough to believe in. Gabriel wondered if such joy were possible off-screen. He checked his watch and realized that he had been walking all day.

He hailed a taxi. When one finally came, he climbed in and leaned forward, "The Ritz-Carlton, Central Park."

The driver nodded and pulled into traffic. Gabriel observed the passersby through a greasy window — couples, groups, people walking alone — how many of them knew a sense of peace and purpose? He arrived at the hotel and made his way to the Star Lounge. Outside the doors, he smiled in an effort to look happy, hoping it would help. The merger and acquisition team were already inside with Michael — all of them in high spirits.

Michael rose from the table and greeted Gabriel with a hug. "We did it!"

Between all the backslapping and handshakes, Gabriel smiled, hoping to become similarly enthusiastic. He still felt nothing. When his salmon steak came, he ate little of it, listening to everyone's chatter of dream vacations and toys.

"So, Gabriel, what are *you* going to do now?" One of the team was smiling in encouragement.

Gabriel looked up from his plate without focusing on anything. "What *am* I going to do now?"

The waiter came with a dessert menu, and Gabriel left not long after. He could not pretend to have joy. He took the elevator up to his suite and filled the deep, soaking tub, hoping to relax and celebrate his victory alone. He cranked up the tub's jets and sat in the roar of foaming water, but instead of feeling any sense of triumph, he felt tears running down his face. The lack of joy shattered his heart. He felt like he was breaking.

Then he knew.

He turned off the tub's jets and let the stillness surround him. He had labored under the false belief that work's success would mean freedom. No external success, not even his present financial windfall, was going to quench the thirst of his life search. As his tears continued, Gabriel asked aloud the questions that live in the hearts of all human beings: "Why am I alive? What is my real purpose? What is true success?"

He heard no answer.

He could not rest until he had searched out the truth. Thoreau's comment in *Walden* about "masses of men leading lives of quiet desperation"[1] plagued him. Was he leading such a life? And then there were the business successes and failures of others. The failures had always haunted him. Gabriel could not get the stories out of his mind. Many friends had made it, yet most were lost in addiction, divorce, or an overall sense of what they described as emptiness.

Gabriel scanned his memory, hoping. . . . Yes, he did remember encountering a few men and women who seemed to walk in a certain kind of life victory, an inner peace. *How did they arrive at business success and peace?* He pressed on, believing that asking the right questions would produce the right answers. He felt hope begin to build. An answer emerged, resonating throughout his person. *Maybe work achievement is not the answer itself, but simply an arena to help me learn the answer. If my business journey is part of my life journey, how can I learn my true reason for being through my life and my work?*

The bath water was getting cold. Gabriel looked down at his feet and saw that his toes resembled the prunes his grandmother had eaten to aid digestion. He laughed and felt the possibility of joy for the first time that day. He reached for a fluffy white hotel robe and walked into the suite's living room. Grabbing his journal and a pen, he sank into the plush, blue sofa.

Not knowing exactly where to start, he decided to simply free write: *We view life through the lenses of our own stories, so to prepare for change; I want to understand my story better. I will look at where I've been, where I am now, and where I want to go. Maybe doing this will help me truly define success.* Gabriel reread those brief lines, satisfied. Gaining confidence, he added: *Discovering the root cause of my restlessness may guide me to its solution.* He was now focused on transforming his temporary life breakdown into a permanent life breakthrough.

Ever the businessman, Gabriel decided to inventory his life: he would take account of every significant event that had already occurred and then project everything that he believed would come. A high-tech version of Dickens' Ghost of Christmas Past, Present, and Yet to Come began to form in his mind's eye. Gabriel began to let his mind skip backward through memories as if he were navigating scene menus on a DVD. He clicked back to his eighth-grade year. That was the year he first began to explore the big ideas about life and love.

The God of Childhood

Holding his father's hand, Gabriel entered the sterile, dim hospital room. The chaplain was standing next to a bed where Gabriel's mother lay, almost lifeless. Gabriel swallowed. The air felt thick in the room and in his soul. He had known that his mother was sick, but he had not known how close to death she was. The chaplain began to minister the last rites.

Gabriel looked up at his father's face, hoping to find hope or any emotion that would help him know how he *should* feel in that moment. His father's face was filled with a still and desperate love for his wife. Gabriel's father, Perino, was normally a highly energetic man. He lived the Italian theme of "La Famiglia" and was fiercely loyal not only to family but also to the Catholic church. A survivor of the Great Depression, he was driven by a relentless work ethic. Work was Perino's burning passion. Gabriel knew that he could please his father by finishing his chores with excellence and speed and by helping out with any of Perino's work.

Gabriel's mother, Mary, was his soul's anchor. If there was a heaven, she was it. She was unconditionally loving by nature and whole-heartedly driven to care for others. His mother was always there for Gabriel — she had pulled giant splinters from his hands and nursed the continual abrasions on his knees. She helped him fix his bicycle, and even cared for his reptilian pets. She seemed to know Christ personally, and Gabriel believed that she lived her faith as fully as humanly possible.

Father Tom from Saint John's Church used to say, "When the time comes, she will go up to heaven like a speeding bullet!" More than anything, Mary desired that her children would come to truly know God. More than getting straight As? Yes. More than making the basketball team? Yes. More than becoming a doctor? Yes.

Both of Gabriel's parents carried a strong, immigrant spirit. In the heartland of central California, they worked hard to support their family and build a life for their children. Family was their ultimate priority.

Gabriel loved his sister, Angela, who was like an angel on earth for the family. But it was his brother, Andrew, who held the heart of the family. Andrew was a special-needs child who lived away from the family in group homes. Visiting Andrew on weekends was a source of great pain and joy for the family.

Gabriel liked to pull Andrew in a wagon, push him on the swing, read to him, and endlessly repeat his made-up words and silly sentences. Loving his brother formed in Gabriel a compassion that eventually enriched and expanded the colors of his own life. Gabriel always noticed the children on the fringe of "normal," and he felt great compassion for them. Through the empathy he felt for Andrew, Gabriel developed a desire to make his own life matter. Andrew became a driving force in Gabriel's life search. Gabriel would say to himself, *Andrew has limited options, but my options are unlimited. I will not waste my life. I will fully invest my life to make a difference!* Andrew also had a gifted sense of the inherent good and evil in people. By observing that in his brother, Gabriel learned to trust his own inner compass.

But in the heavy atmosphere of the hospital room, Gabriel did not know whom or what to trust. His mother, his greatest safe harbor, was under attack. Gabriel could not cry. Despite his deep love for his mother, he was unable to express his pain. Then, out of nowhere, he remembered a school report he had written about *The Diary of a Young Girl* by Anne Frank. Anne was about his age when she wrote the words that translated the state of his heart, there in the hospital room:

> *Today the sun is shining, the sky is a deep blue, there is a lovely breeze and I am longing — so longing — for everything. To talk, for freedom, for friends, to be alone. And I do so long . . . to cry! I feel as if I am going to burst, and I know that it would get better with crying; but I can't. I am restless, I go from one*

room to another, breathe through the crack of a closed window, feel my heart beating, as if it is saying, "Can't you satisfy my longings at last?" I believe that it is spring within me, I feel that spring is awakening, I feel it in my whole body and soul. . . . It is an effort to behave normally. I feel utterly confused. I do not know what to read. What to write. What to do. I only know that I am longing.[2]

Longing. That was it. Gabriel was not even sure what he was longing for. He had always been driven to seek God. *Is that what this longing is?* He could not stop thinking about it.

Lying in bed that night, Gabriel began to pray for his mother's recovery. He drifted off to sleep and dreamed a dazzling dream: his body was catapulted through a dark tunnel. He was in agony as he flew, his form tossing, turning, and tumbling along as if on a path toward death. But then he arrived at a threshold of light. Before him, sunlight streamed through a prism, and the light burst forth into brilliant colors. Everything was so radiant and comforting that it dissolved the fear of the dream's traumatic introduction. He was overcome with joy.

When Gabriel woke up the next morning, he knew he had dreamt about his mother. Though she was close to death, she would experience the light of that dream and come back to him. Gabriel had an inexplicable urge to visit the family's church, Saint John's, before the daily mass began. He wanted to hear directly from heaven. Previously, Saint John's had been a symbolic display of ritual and religion for Gabriel, but now it seemed to be the place to find a sign of reassurance that his mother would live.

He entered the church and ran to the front, kneeling before the altar. For the first time in his life, Gabriel replaced rote prayers for a heartfelt appeal to his Creator. Then it happened. The tears started as a mild burning sensation around his eyes, and then they poured out as if from a wellspring — an untouched place deep within him. When his tears ended, Gabriel felt a sensation begin at his feet and quickly rise through his body until it rested in his heart. Gabriel knew that his mother was healed, but the real breakthrough was that he knew he had been healed as well. He was healed from feeling alone and separated from God.

A week after that miraculous day at Saint John's church, his mother was released from the hospital. Gabriel had experienced an awakening through that life-and-death encounter, and he became intimately connected to the highest form of power and love. When he had needed God most, God had shown up and proven to be more secure than even his mother's love. Gabriel had met the God of his childhood. This intimate encounter was the single greatest epiphany of his young life. Beyond his own comprehension, he had discovered the presence of something or Someone greater than himself. This discovery was certainly part of his life search.

Decades later, Gabriel set his journal down. Looking back at that revelation, he wondered, *Where did God go? Or maybe I should ask, "Where did I go?"* He thought back to the years after that early epiphany.

Sister Grace

Sitting on the blue sofa at the Ritz, Gabriel's right ear tingled as he remembered. He laughed aloud: "Why was it *always* the right ear?" Sister Grace had a habit of yanking his ear from behind when he was not singing during daily mass.

Saint John's also had an elementary school, and Sister Grace was a fixture at both. Gabriel loved Sister Grace, but sometimes he did everything he could to taunt her. She was a powerful woman with gleaming silver hair and fiery blue eyes, and she exuded energy and dedication. She held both the carrot and the stick, but she wielded the stick the most. Even as a boy, Gabriel thought that Sister Grace lived life in a legalistic straightjacket, but he admired her, and she respected him, despite his rebel-with-a-cause antics. His cause was a good-natured desire to see people around him flourishing — something that hours sitting at hard desks did not seem to foster.

One day, Sister Grace was teaching a math class that felt like it was lasting an eternity. Unable to bear another moment, Gabriel climbed up on his desk and started dancing like Elvis. His friends burst into uncontrollable laughter that spread to all the classmates. A girl fell out of her seat, she was laughing so hard. Sister Grace threw a chalkboard eraser at Gabriel. He dodged it, and a cloud of white chalk exploded as the eraser hit the back wall. The laughter grew louder.

In an era of corporal punishment, Sister Grace's flying eraser was a painless and entertaining consequence. Even though he had experienced the more traditional punishments now and then, Gabriel realized now that the culture of discipline had produced an environment of freedom in which the students could explore. By setting boundaries, Sister Grace actually encouraged Gabriel's exploration beyond them.

During his years at Saint John's, Gabriel continued to learn the freedom to experiment within a hierarchical system. His good grades also earned him extra freedom. His father, Perino, used Gabriel's love of dirt bike riding and basketball as an incentive to ensure his academic excellence. It was much easier to get through algebra homework while anticipating the trails. On his dirt bike,

Gabriel's mind could change channels from analytical to visceral as he zoomed across the landscape at high speeds. Then there were the rigorous basketball practices and competitions. It all added up to a life of disciplined freedom. As Gabriel's mind and body were being trained, so was his spirit.

One of his responsibilities at Saint John's was altar serving. Holding the cross steady in front of him, Gabriel would lead the procession into church for Mass. He enjoyed the responsibility, and he knew he looked dignified in the red-and-white altar boy vestments. He also mastered the art of not crying while the perfumed incense smoke swirled around his eyes. Holy Communion was Gabriel's favorite part of the ceremony. The internal condition of his heart and mind changed in the presence of the sacred remembrance. To Gabriel, such rituals meant much more than fulfilling a duty at church; he had encountered the source that inspired them through his dream and his mother's miraculous recovery. After that experience, Gabriel felt more alive. Questions about life and death were growing in the soil of his mind.

He did not understand how, but death seemed to be an ally to life. He was continually drawn to solve the mystery of death. During funerals at Saint John's, he had a front row seat as an altar server. After the services, Gabriel would try to figure out why people wanted to look at a lifeless body in a casket. If a person died after living a full life, and if he was *really* going to heaven, shouldn't his relatives and friends be celebrating instead of mourning?

One day, Gabriel and his friend Christopher snuck into the mortuary adjacent to the church. Lying right there on the table was a dead body! This corpse was more real and terrifying than the bodies all dressed up in coffins. The boys crept closer. Suddenly, the arm of the recently embalmed body shifted and made a creaking sound. Adrenaline surged in Gabriel and Christopher as they set a new world record for the twenty-yard dash while fleeing the mortuary.

Gabriel discovered that funerals and funeral homes were not only good for asking the big questions or having fun; they were also lucrative. At one particular funeral, a family member of the deceased gave Gabriel a white envelope. It felt like it was burning a hole in his pocket as he politely waited for the service to end before opening it. His mind raced with the possibilities of its contents. When the altar boys had finished the recessional and were gathering in the vestry, Gabriel tore open the envelope.

He gasped, "Alleluia!"

Two, crisp twenty-dollar bills rested inside. One afternoon of funeral service had exceeded the total earnings of Gabriel's fourteenth birthday party. Realizing that working funerals could be a profitable business, Gabriel began to serve at every funeral scheduled at Saint John's. To mix it up, he also served at weddings and events where those being celebrated still lived in their physical bodies. He was becoming keenly aware of compound interest and was intent on growing his savings account, much to his father's delight. Life, death, God, motorcycles, basketball, and visions of money swirled around his mind. The seeds of Spirit and the spirit of entrepreneurship were beginning to grow together.

Sometimes, Gabriel would get lost in the unexplored and infinite galaxies of his mind while on his life search. Perhaps because he was not even sure what he was searching for, he would become completely exhausted as he reached beyond his ability to grasp the depth of his inner thoughts. When Sister Grace taught on Saint Augustine's life, Gabriel paid close attention. He was intrigued by what the saint had written in his book *Confessions*: "You have made us for yourself, Lord, and our hearts are restless until they rest in you."[3]

There it was again: *Restless*. Gabriel shifted on the couch, trying to catch up with his own thoughts in his journal. Even as an adult, Gabriel wanted to know what Saint Augustine meant — what rest meant. Like the business strategist he was, Gabriel longed to connect the dots from yesterday's lessons to today so that he could have a better tomorrow. But a certain memory interrupted that logical thought process.

The First Kiss

Gabriel remembered asking himself, "What would it be like? What could be better than kissing a girl?" Since the opportunity had not presented itself by age fourteen, Gabriel decided to go out and make his first kiss happen. First, he would need a girl. He thought his friend Isabella might be willing. Second, he would need the perfect venue. The church. Yes, Saint John's would be perfect, and surely the kiss would be holy there. Plus, he and Isabella would be conveniently close to the altar and the confessional.

After school, Gabriel found Isabella on the playground. He waved her over to where he was standing. She smiled and hopped off the bench where she was sitting with her friends.

Gabriel shoved his hands in his pockets and asked, "Would you like to try something new?"

Isabella tilted her head, "What?"

Gabriel looked around to make sure no one was within earshot. He whispered, "Do you want to try kissing?"

She giggled, "Sure."

"Meet me in the church tomorrow after school."

The next morning Gabriel wanted to look his best. Deciding what to wear was easy since all Saint John's students wore uniforms; nevertheless, Gabriel carefully selected a pair of military green pants free of iron-on knee patches and a clean, white shirt. Most importantly, he wore his new Converse® Chuck Taylor All Stars. During all of his classes that day, Gabriel considered the kiss. Would it feel strange? Would he fall in love? Would he become wiser? Would it be a piece of his life search? Sister Grace did not have to worry about him distracting class. He was already distracted.

After school Gabriel entered the quiet church. The stained glass windows magnified the sunlight streaming inside. The inner sanctum was aglow in the light of the altar and prayer candles. Gabriel smiled. He had chosen the perfect romantic atmosphere. And there was Isabella. She was sitting on the front pew. She seemed to be glowing. She looked radiant in her plaid, military green skirt and crisp, white blouse. "*Wow,*" thought Gabriel. "*If the actual kiss is anything like* thinking *about the kiss, this is going to be the best day of my life!*" He crossed himself and walked up the aisle to sit next to Isabella.

Neither said a word. Speaking only with their eyes, they slowly moved their lips toward each other's. Their heads drew closer. Their lips came together at the same time, touching for a nanosecond...

They shot apart.

Isabella blushed, and Gabriel smiled in relief. Still silent, they realized that they were in way over their heads. Now several feet apart, they each slumped back in the pew and started laughing. Gabriel said, "OK, maybe we can wait awhile."

Isabella nodded, "Want to work on our history homework?"

They finished all of their homework there on the hard pew.

Many years and kisses later, Gabriel lay back on the soft sofa in the executive suite at the Ritz and took in the marble, the fine fabrics, the exotic flowers. Everything spoke to material success. Nothing spoke to relational success. Gabriel was there alone. His family members were not there to celebrate with him, nor did he desire for them to be. He had to figure something out first, or he would not be able to be there for his family even if he was in the same room with them.

Gabriel did not remember falling asleep. He woke on the sofa the next morning, stiff and famished. He ordered room service and got dressed. He ate his veggie omelet, so preoccupied with the thoughts from the day before that he barely noticed the perfect texture and flavor of the eggs. He stared out across the green trees of Central Park.

Gabriel realized that the doors were now open between his past, present, and future. Something deep within was coaxing him forward on a journey that he knew to be his life search. He also knew, instinctively, that it would be a journey of agony *and* ecstasy. To think more clearly, he needed fresh air and a walk. Another lesson of Sister Grace's surfaced: *Solvitur ambulando:* "It is solved by walking."

He grabbed his coat and left his room. When he stepped into the hotel corridor, he froze. A maid's cart, full of fresh towels, trash bags, soap, and miniature bottles of shampoo lined up like little soldiers was slowly inching toward him. No one was pushing it. Gabriel wondered if he might be losing his mind. Then a gray head appeared above the rim of the cart. An extremely petite, elderly woman was pushing the cart by leveraging her body toward it at an acute angle. Gabriel paused as she passed by, and his heart filled with compassion.

"Pardon me," he asked, "What is your name?"

The woman looked up at him with a smile, pleased that he had taken the time to speak to her. She said, "Naomi."

She reminded Gabriel of his immigrant grandmother, Nonna. He shook her hand. "Thank you for your work."

"You are most welcome," she said, continuing forward, angled into the cart, her work. Gabriel watched her move slowly down the hall. *I, too, have become invisible as I push my work cart. Something has to change.* Yet, unbeknownst to Gabriel, something *was* changing.

Gabriel thanked the elevator conductor. He thanked the doorman who opened the glass doors into a breezy morning. He stopped to put money into a homeless man's hat at the entrance to Central Park. He walked along the park's path, trying to make eye contact with everyone he passed. Most people looked away, absorbed in their own worlds. After a while, Gabriel stopped at a large rock and sat on it.

He asked no one in particular, "What has happened to the God of my childhood?" That God was the one who had answered Gabriel's childhood life search questions with promises like, "Yes, there is more to your life. Yes, there is Someone greater who walks with you. Yes, your life will be great." Gabriel breathed in deeply as he reminded himself of these words. He longed for the peace beyond understanding he had once known. He longed for something more than money and titles on a business card. Heaven had rescued him that morning at Saint John's when he knew his mother's life was spared. Even though he was just a child, he had discovered a secret place of wisdom. He longed to revisit that place where innocence and trust meet to form joy and love.

Adrenaline and Hormones

Somewhere between the fourteen-year-old boy and the man sitting on a rock in Central Park, Gabriel had lost that innocence. As Gabriel continued his life inventory, he cringed a bit while recalling his late teens and early twenties when his life was ruled by the god of adrenaline and hormones.

He had been attending college when she happened — the girl from his biology class. They were lab partners, and that morning they had sat agonizingly elbow to elbow, studying germs under a microscope. Later that afternoon at the athletics complex, she walked toward him on the green and playfully pulled at his sweaty shirt.

"So how many germ varieties live on *this?*"

He smiled, but no words came out. *"Yikes! What's happening to me?"* The only thing that he could think about was tackling her and gnawing on her calf.

Ever since his first kiss with Isabella, Gabriel had loved the very concept of the female species. Their outer beauty was alluring, but their inner beauty was captivating. He had been raised to respect women and to find one (and only one) to share his life with, but Gabriel never did like the rules of math. One was not enough for him. That afternoon, the girl from biology class invited Gabriel back to her dorm room.

Like the cell division he was studying that first semester, Gabriel's explorations began to multiply exponentially. Looking back from the present, Gabriel saw that life season as a version of the *Odyssey* by Homer. In the Greek epic poem, the Sirens played their enchanting songs, causing the sailors to steer their vessels into the rocks; however, in Gabriel's edition, the Sirens grew legs and attended all of his classes at university. He was not yet mature enough to resist the song of temptation. Like the sailors in the epic, he veered off course and crashed onto the rocks. During this phase of life, he traversed the slippery slope of sexuality without spirituality.

And here he was now, sitting on a rock instead of destroying himself against one. Had he figured anything out? He looked at the dark mass of stone beneath him, feeling the solidity of it. He thought of another kind of rock from Scripture — the kind that acted as an anchor instead of a demolisher. *Maybe I would not have crashed if I had asked Him in advance what He thought about my life choices.*

In that moment, Gabriel remembered the Old Testament story of King David and Bathsheba. Witnessing Bathsheba's beauty in the moonlight, David had been overcome with jealousy and desire. He placed her husband, Uriah, on the front lines of battle to ensure his death. It was not until the prophet Nathan pointed out David's destructive behavior that the truth of David's actions caused him to be full of grief and heartache. Like David, Gabriel had placed his own will ahead of God's will. Like David, Gabriel had broken his heavenly Father's heart with an act of pride. Like David, Gabriel remembered desperately crying out for mercy and forgiveness; and, like David, Gabriel knew the process of restoration was possible.

"*Perhaps,*" he thought, "*our decisions must be filtered through something greater than ourselves.*" Gabriel jumped off the rock and continued to wander through Central Park. He stopped by a vendor's stand

and bought a pretzel for lunch, feeling drawn to the shape that mirrored his thoughts.

He approached the Bow Bridge where a homeless woman was sitting with her hand held out. Gabriel stopped to carefully place two, twenty-dollar bills into her hands. She had the most empty and hopeless eyes that he had ever seen.

Hope. That was something he had finally seen realized in the realm of love twenty years ago. He was glad to leave behind memories of loveless relationships for the most loving one he had ever known.

The Responsible Brother

The Bridge

Gabriel walked to the middle of the Bow Bridge and crossed into a memory that caused him to smile. They had met on a bridge in spring. The sun had just broken through a heavy rainstorm. The creek beneath rushed with its new waters. Gabriel did not hear the water. He had seen her. She walked toward him from the opposite side of the bridge. Her hair was blond, and it seemed to glow in the bright light. But instead of a purely physical reaction to her beauty, Gabriel felt something different; new. He felt a reaction to her spirit. His spirit connected with hers.

Time stopped. The cherry blossoms sparkled. Her smile sparkled. The world — his included — seemed washed and refreshed. Looking into her blue eyes transported him to a place where *any*thing was possible. Standing in her presence was like being planted next to a flowing stream of water.

All of a sudden, he could hear the creek again. He could hear himself say, "Hello."

She stopped a few feet away and said, "Hello."

He felt fourteen years old again and shoved his hands in the pockets of his coat, meaning to ask her something — anything — to keep her from walking by. He decided to introduce himself.

Pulling his hand from his pocket, he started, "I am ...," but the coat fabric seemed to be fighting him, and when he yanked his hand out, his keys were attached. They went flying into the creek. That was certainly one way to prolong the encounter. Gabriel looked into the water and back at the lovely woman in front of him. This time his hand made contact with hers. "I am Gabriel."

"And you are missing some keys. My name is Tirzah."

"*Tirrrzzzaaahhh...*" Gabriel felt soothed as he slowly let her name roll off his tongue. He realized he was staring deeply into her eyes when her brows lifted. He tried to gather himself together. "Um, I guess ... How deep is that creek? I wonder if they...?"

He leaned over the worn wooden railing of the bridge, feeling her arm near his. She was also looking into the water.

She pointed, "There."

Sure enough, a shimmery reflection made it through the water not too far from the creek bank. His keys. Gabriel ran off the bridge and stood on the grassy bank that reached right up to the water. Barely within arm's reach, his keys rested between two stones. Gabriel pulled off his jacket and tossed it beneath him on the soaked grass, rolling up his sleeves. He lay on his jacket and began to lean toward the water.

Tirzah, who had come up beside him, said, "If you lean too far, you will fall in. Here." And with that, she knelt down and held his ankles.

More or less anchored, Gabriel was able to balance his weight and reach his keys, only soaking the upper part of his rolled sleeves.

And thus, the tone of their relationship was set: Mr. Creativity and Risk met Miss Grounded and Organizational. The perfect business partners. The perfect life partners. Tirzah's character was strong and her mind sharp. She was open and real and lived up to her name, which means: "she is my delight," in Hebrew. Tirzah's fortitude was evident, considering that she stuck with Gabriel after their first date, during which he got a reckless driving ticket and lost his license. They married twelve months after graduating college.

After a brief panic attack at his new responsibilities, the newly wedded Gabriel decided that he needed a mentor and selected his uncle Patrick, a successful entrepreneur and former Fortune 500 vice president. Within months of marriage, Gabriel was laser-focused on work. He began his professional career as a sales representative for a computer company in southern California.

Title and Money

As a sales representative, Gabriel had officially started his climb up the imaginary ladder he affectionately called the ladder of title and money. Gabriel smiled as he remembered his first assignment at the computer company. After nine months of intense technology training, he was finally given the keys to the demo van. The demo van was actually a small motor home filled with high-end computer equipment to mobilize technology demonstrations.

After a cautious trial run, Gabriel felt confident to begin.

He set out for his first client. Excited, he sped into an intersection, taking a sharp right turn too fast. The $100,000 van leaned onto its right wheels, its left ones completely lifting off the pavement. Gabriel's career flashed before his eyes. "*This is it! It's all over.*" But he reacted fast, corrected the van, and averted a rollover. After his lungs filled with air again, Gabriel vowed to stay focused in his new world of greater responsibility.

When not driving the demo van, Gabriel worked in an open office environment with eleven other sales representatives. He engaged his customers via the telephone and always exceeded his quota, yet he felt somewhat inferior surrounded by his coworkers with their degrees from brand-name universities. One thing drove his passion to succeed: the sales board directly in front of him. Every employee's name was listed on that board in order of sales achievement. As the rookie, Gabriel's name was last. That placement was like throwing gasoline on a fire.

Each morning Gabriel reminded himself of his seemingly impossible goal: to be at the top of the board in one year. The fierce work ethic he had inherited from his father drove him toward his goal. As if Perino were still standing over his shoulder examining the quality of his chores, Gabriel felt a constant drive to do more and do better. After extra hours, miles, and smiles in the office and demo van: mission accomplished! Gabriel was named rookie of the year and even received a gift of tickets to the Olympics. His professional career was up and running.

One day after his typical whirlwind of tension-filled, high-stakes work, Gabriel got a call that had nothing to do with sales. His friend Mark was at the hospital. Mark was larger than life - strong and capable in everything he did - but his wife had just given birth to a premature baby who lay in an incubator fighting for his life.

Mark's voice retained its strength on the other end of the phone as he simply told Gabriel, "The baby isn't doing well."

Gabriel was already grabbing his briefcase with one hand, "I'll be right there."

He sped to the hospital, where the receptionist pointed him to the neonatal ICU. Standing next to his friend in front of rows of infants on the brink between life and death, Gabriel's work world receded. *"Why do you think that your work is a matter of life and death?"* Gabriel was not sure if he had asked himself that question or if something — someone — else had. The question lodged in his heart, reawakening the hunger of his life search. Hadn't he been feeding it with his climb up the ladder of title and money? As he watched Mark's baby fight to live, he was not sure.

Gabriel had been consumed with an upward, linear career path to reach the same height as his uncle and mentor, Patrick. He had truly believed that such fulfillment would be comprehensive. He was beginning to suspect otherwise.

Thankfully, the baby not only lived but also thrived. Gabriel returned to work, setting aside thoughts of anything else. It was not long before he proved his sales abilities. Job offers began rolling in, and he accepted a lucrative offer to be a sales manager for another technology company. Now responsible for the welfare of others, Gabriel treated his work with even greater care.

The position suited him. He loved each member of his team and desired to encourage their individual life success as well as the team's combined work success. Gabriel had discovered his gift to unselfishly mine the gold in others, refine it, and help make it beautiful and useful beyond itself. His teams thrived in a culture of trust, encouragement, accountability, and mentoring as they set new sales growth records.

Gabriel was quickly promoted to national sales director and added to an exclusive mentoring program where he received cross-training in marketing, finance, and human resources. His mentor, Mr. Douglas, was the CFO of the company. Mr. Douglas was a chiseled, no-nonsense ex-marine. A picture of General Patton hung behind his desk, flanked by the flags of America and California. Through Mr. Douglas's example, Gabriel began to see business as a battle to be won. Mr. Douglas would bellow, "Your ultimate security is your ability to produce!" and "Do not confuse efforts with results!" This motto was echoed by one of Patton's own that Gabriel had heard before: "A good plan violently executed today is better than a perfect plan next week." And so, with each new victory, Gabriel became more and more ambitious about conquering the battlefield of business.

Meanwhile, Tirzah had joined a leading technology company and was also succeeding in the workplace. She and Gabriel were both small town kids in the big city. They burned, like their immigrant parents, to conquer this new land of opportunity. They agreed to be hyper-disciplined and started a process called Freedom Book to ensure focus and accountability on their life priorities, most of which were work-centric at the time.

The couple successfully managed their marriage like a business. The family was the corporation, and they each had a clearly communicated role for its advancement. The spillover benefit was in the form of dedicated meetings for communication and conflict resolution. With the business of family well managed, Gabriel and Tirzah could freely enjoy the other aspects of their romance together.

A key component of their Freedom Book was finances. Gabriel and Tirzah formed a covenant early in their marriage that budgets and investments were akin to employees in their family corporation and would need to be productive. They were fiscally conservative and even outfitted their home with used furniture from Gabriel's office. They were also wise, despite the risk, to invest in information technology, riding the crest of that sector's stock market wave.

Gabriel's experience with the ladder of title and money was easily measured quantitatively. *Maybe this is why so many people define success by these metrics,* he thought to himself. His father's experiences during the Great Depression had driven him to earn and save in an insatiable way. Having enough money was supposed to insulate him from all fear, yet it was fear that haunted him and propelled the unhealthy part of his ambition — the fear of not doing enough or having enough security. The overactive need for security drove him to create the illusion of security.

And so, every few years, Gabriel was promoted further up the chain of command. Sometimes, his title exceeded his maturity level, but he was savvy and always found a way to get the job done well.

Gabriel felt that he could will anything to happen. Even when Perino told him that he had been diagnosed with cancer, Gabriel felt he could fix it. He advised his father on treatments and health plans and sent him a large package filled with every kind of expensive vitamin, green powder, and herbal supplement. Not long after sending the package, Gabriel and Tirzah visited Perino and Mary. When Tirzah opened the cupboard to make tea, she found all of the supplements untouched, crammed into the shelves.

"Perino, you haven't used any of these," she chided with a smile.

Perino smiled back. "I found something better."

Mary laughed, "Yes. Show them what you found."

Perino opened another cupboard. There sat the largest box of Total® cereal Gabriel and Tirzah had ever seen. The box read: "100% Daily Value of 12 Vitamins and Minerals." Tirzah smiled at Perino's innocence and willpower.

As Perino successfully fought the cancer into remission, barely missing a day of work while eating many bowls of cereal, Gabriel battled through every issue that arose in his own life. And his life equaled his work. Gabriel had a gift for seeing new and imaginative solutions to problems. Executives saw his innovation in turnaround projects. He was a revolutionary, relative to the status quo, and enjoyed the challenge of positive change. Still starting something new or turning it around required a massive amount of energy. He often worked seventy hours per week while also traveling around the world.

Gabriel taught himself the business etiquette for each country he visited. While in Taiwan, he learned more about the power of relationships, or *Guanxi*, a critical success factor in Taiwanese culture and one that Gabriel began to implement in his domestic business deals. Business was competitive but great fun to Gabriel. Mr. Jerred, his company's CEO, would often say that work was play with a purpose.

It was an exciting adventure for Gabriel to identify his customers' pain points and solve them while still earning a profit. He thrived on finding the strategic advantage and enjoying the sweet taste of victory. Overall, he found it exhilarating to simply get the right things done and done well. Excellence became its own reward and afforded Gabriel the opportunity to enjoy some of the perks of his industry: front row seats at the Super Bowl, flights on private jets, and presidential suites. His name appeared in Top 50 lists. The phone started ringing.

At home, Gabriel and Tirzah continued to carefully execute their Freedom Book plan. It was time for family expansion, but they would need to change their partner job descriptions. Gabriel would be responsible for the family's income. Tirzah would be the chief operating officer of their growing family venture. To seal the deal, they invested in the safest family car available at the time: a Volvo.

Tirzah gave birth to two children. First came Terese. She was the very spirit of life seeking life, overflowing with love and power. Her creativity, curiosity, and authority were extraordinary. Then came Daniel. He was a pure wellspring of wisdom and dominion from the beginning. His heart was majestic, strong and gentle. Gabriel's children became his great joy, far above his work.

"Finally," thought Gabriel. *"This is it: wife, children, work. I am fulfilled. Right?"*

But he was not. That now-annoying thirst and hunger for his life search seemed even stronger. Gabriel painfully realized that the ladder he had so diligently climbed had become a false god for life fulfillment.

Religion and Social Justice

Gabriel had reached the peak of anything anyone could want, and yet he felt broken, instead of whole. It was as if the restlessness in him had increased to the point that it shattered him. If he had it all but did not feel fulfilled, what could bring total satisfaction and rest? Gabriel reached out to the god of religion and social justice and this became his newest ladder to climb.

He went to the confessional at The Cathedral of Saint Francis

By-the-Sea in Laguna Beach and sat in the dim light as the priest made the prayer of the sign of the cross. Gabriel remained silent.

Eventually, the priest asked, "What sins have you committed, my son?"

Gabriel felt an ache gnawing inside him as he admitted in a whisper. "I do not trust God. Help me to trust God."

This time the priest was silent.

Gabriel dropped his head into his hands and wept. He had thought that God would be in his — Gabriel's — success. Almost envious of the priest and his purpose, Gabriel walked out of the church. On the sidewalk, he turned back and looked at the building. Maybe he needed to work directly for God in the church and workplace.

Gabriel and Tirzah quickly became lectors, Eucharistic ministers, and family ministry leaders at Saint Francis. Gabriel so enjoyed the life and writings of Saint Francis that he traveled to Assisi, Italy, to study his life. His family began serving at the local soup kitchen. Gabriel even took a sabbatical to help a nonprofit Christian organization prepare and execute a new business plan. Like anything man-made, religion had its pure-hearted followers and its hypocrites. Gabriel's deep longing to trust in something beyond himself grew even more profound. He believed that there was a powerful step he must take on this new ladder.

One day, while handing out pieces of cornbread at the soup kitchen, Gabriel looked into the eyes of the man in front of him. He was holding his tray out in hunger, but something in the man's spirit spoke to Gabriel of other hungers. Gabriel became intrigued with the plight of the homeless and decided to spend twenty-four hours at a homeless shelter to talk with the men living there. Their stories humbled him:

"I lost my home in a bad business deal."

"I cheated on my wife. She left and took everything. I deserve it."

"Got in a fight with my dad a few years ago. He kicked me out. Haven't tried going back."

Gabriel sat on the edge of the stained bed he had been given, in exchange for a sizeable donation to the shelter. His privilege and favor felt like a burden there in the only home the hopeless, sweat-stained men knew. So many of them were there because of a single bad decision that had drastically changed their lives.

At home the next evening over dinner, Daniel looked up from his chicken and asked his father, "Why did you stay with the homeless people when you have a home?"

Terese looked at her father, "What did you do there?"

Gabriel met Tirzah's eyes across the full table. The plenty of his life was magnified after the previous night. He looked at each of his children and smiled, "I wanted to understand what it feels like to not have this. We are so blessed. I did not want to forget that."

After helping with the dishes, Gabriel retreated to his room and sat on the soft, clean bed he shared with his beautiful wife in the lovely home they had created for their children. *Am I a good father to them? Am I loving them well?* And then the question that hurt the most: *Do I know how to love well?* Despite the contrasted bounty and love he was able to enjoy in his home — or maybe because of it — Gabriel hated himself for the never-ending restlessness within himself. All of the philanthropy and volunteerism were only Band-Aids® stuck to a broken spirit. It was true that Gabriel had grown in compassion and love while helping others, yet he hungered for his own rescue from his "achieve-aholic" mentality.

He did not have time to think much more about his life search. Not long after the night spent at the homeless shelter, Gabriel was poised on the threshold of his greatest career opportunity to date. He was promoted to a position as vice president of a Fortune 500 company. His first assignment in his new role was to turn around and grow a recent corporate acquisition. Success would lead him into a broad-based leadership role on a global stage. As usual, he worked around the clock with his team and advisory council. The acquisition wildly exceeded all expectations. It also set a new industry standard for how to build a value-added business community.

So far Gabriel had been able to remain apolitical, but now he was working for larger, highly political organizations. As land is a mystery to fish, so were bureaucrats to an entrepreneur. He was shocked to learn that not everyone puts the corporate vision first. He struggled with self-promoters whose personal ambitions were ahead of the company's vision, and he was irritated by bureaucrats who elevated their positions ahead of the company's core purpose.

The company's CEO, however, appreciated Gabriel's pioneering spirit and would often select him to lead the new and controversial projects that threatened to shift power. With protection from the top, Gabriel embraced the role of a disruptive change agent to help the company take new ground.

Although he was now a vice president with power and influence, Gabriel longed to be free of corporate constraints. A desire was growing to find and unite a select team of "A" players to change the world.

The Impossible Dream Made Possible

The coffee shop table overlooked the California coastline. Michael held up his empty cappuccino mug and clinked it on Gabriel's. Both men looked out at the ocean, drawn to things larger than they could imagine. On a napkin between them was a concept sketch for a mobile application that would transform user experience of smart phones.

Michael was a close friend and a cognitive science/human computer interaction graduate from the University of California, San Diego. He and Gabriel had spent the last hour casting a dream for a new business.

Gabriel smiled. "Here's to *Voice Innovation International*."

They prepared a business plan and invested $183,000 of their savings into the start-up. *Voice Innovation International's* first worldwide headquarters began in a small retail shopping mall next to a blood bank. Michael became friends with Ava, a phlebotomist who worked there. Against her better judgment, Ava agreed to a crazy idea that Michael had; she drew blood from the two founders and gave the vials to them for a somewhat unique form of inspiration. Literally and figuratively, Gabriel and Michael put their blood, sweat, and tears into the start-up.

The new business was a result of what Gabriel called "spirit streaming." This was simply the revelation and activation of vision. The words of his start-up mentor, Charles, also rang in his ears: "Vision without execution is hallucination." Gabriel and Michael certainly executed their vision, which was continually before them: an innovative user experience that would empower all people to have simple access to information.

In the early days of owning and operating their own business, the two men often had no clue what to do next. They learned to simply walk one step at a time by faith. Their vision, perseverance, and market timing paid off. Within three years, the start-up grew into a seventeen-million-dollar business run by twenty-nine team members. The business's success far surpassed the founders' initial dream in the beachside coffee shop. In fact, their company did so well that it caught the attention of a larger company.

And just yesterday, Gabriel and Michael had actually closed the deal, selling *Voice Innovation International* for a celebratory figure. But it was a success that brought no closure to Gabriel's life search.

The inventory of these pivot points in his life brought Gabriel back to the present. He found himself having wandered obliviously through Harlem to the northern tip of Manhattan Island. The parallel was not lost on him: he had walked to the end of the land, and he had climbed to the top of his external ladders. Looking out over the Hudson River, Gabriel thought, *I arrived at the summit of both life ladders, but my life search has only grown more desperate than before. Now what?*

The Rest-Giving Father

The Ultimate Promotion

Gabriel did not have to wait long for an answer. He had returned to the hotel and had barely been seated for dinner that evening when his mobile phone rang.

Tirzah's voice was strong and gentle: "Your father is in the hospital. Your mother isn't well, and she can't make the three-hour trip to be with him."

Gabriel stood up and was halfway out the door before he finished his reply, "I'll catch the red-eye. I am on my way."

Gabriel was back in California the next morning. He did not even go home but went straight to the hospital: Room number 296. This time, instead of standing by his dying mother, Gabriel stood by his dying father.

When the doctor arrived, he explained that the cancer had not only returned but had also spread. Perino had successfully defeated the cancer for five years. This was different. Perino's vital signs were failing rapidly.

Gabriel was Perino's health care advocate and held the power of attorney. The doctor handed him a DNR (Do Not Resuscitate) form to authorize. Gabriel took the form but could not think about signing it. When the doctor left, Gabriel sat heavily by his father's bedside, more concerned with heavenly matters than legal ones. As if sensing the shift, his father woke and simply looked at his son. Gabriel reached for his father's hand. It felt like sandpaper from all of its years of labor. It was a strong hand.

Gabriel asked, "Are you ready for the afterlife?"

Perino gripped his son's hand: "I need your help to get there."

An immigrant, Perino knew the importance of asking for help to enter a new country. He knew that his son had spent this life searching for the key to the next one. Even so, Gabriel marveled that his father, the patriarch of a staunch, Catholic family should ask him for help. Though he had been active in the church all of his life, Perino was not sure he would make it to heaven.

Gabriel entered a spirit-knowing state that he could barely express in words. He knew a father's love for his own father. He knew that this love came from a source beyond either one of them. And Gabriel knew that he was the one to help his earthly father meet his heavenly one. Perino's grip loosened as he fell back asleep. Gabriel had real accountability beyond the form in his hand.

Perino remained asleep, and Gabriel informed the doctor that he would take the risk and respond to the DNR the next day. That evening Gabriel went to the hospital chapel to pray. He was moved by the stained glass image of a shepherd caring for his sheep. A Bible verse below the window read, "Nothing can separate us from the love of God, not even death." These words gave him new hope that Perino's life would end on the highest note possible.

The following morning, Gabriel returned to room 296 only to find it empty. His heart tightened. *"Where is Dad?"* His mind raced through the options. He anxiously asked the nurse in charge. She smiled and pointed to a hallway between two wings of the oncology floor. As Gabriel looked through the small window in the door, he witnessed an image of fortitude that would be forever inscribed in his mind. Perino, wearing only a pale green hospital gown, was willing himself forward step by step, pulling his IV cart back and forth in the hallway. *"I will never complain about minor aches and pains again,"* Gabriel thought to himself. Perino was doing laps in the hallway in an attempt to regain strength. His vital signs had miraculously improved during the night. He greeted Gabriel with a warm smile and the light of hope in his eye.

Gabriel conferred with the doctor, who said the improvement was only temporary and that Perino's time was short. The medical team released him from the hospital to spend his final days at home. Gabriel did not have the heart to share the prognosis with his father. They checked out of the hospital and embarked on the three-hour journey to his parents' home. During the drive, Perino told stories of his life, including details that Gabriel had never heard. Perino's father had died from the effects of being gassed in World War I. Perino had been nine years old at the time and had to go to work as a caddy to help put food on the table for a family of seven.

Perino looked down at his shoes, "One time, I waited in line for four hours to get a new pair of shoes. Some social welfare program. When my turn came, they looked at my shoes and said, 'No, the hole in the sole is only the size of a dime.' Had to be the size of a quarter to get a new pair. That day I vowed to have work for the rest of my life."

The hole in the sole. The hole in the soul. Gabriel looked at his father sitting in the passenger seat. "Yesterday you asked me to help you get to the other side."

Perino nodded, watching the desert through the window. "I love God, but I am not sure God loves me."

Perino had spent his entire life as a devout Catholic but was still not certain what his eternal address would be.

Instead of confirming that God *did* love his father, Gabriel said, "God is not mad at you."

Perino looked down his hands. As if seeing all of the faithful work they had done, he seemed able to accept that God was not angry with him. Gabriel watched him out of the corner of his eye, almost able to read his father's thoughts.

Perino smiled, "Well, maybe He does not think I am too bad."

Gabriel smiled back, "Maybe He loves you no matter what . . . just like you love me."

"Maybe I did not know how to love you so well."

Gabriel knew that was his father's way of asking forgiveness, and he was filled with gratitude — both for the request and the chance to give it.

"Maybe I did not know how to love you so well, either."

They each looked hard out the windshield. Gabriel began to see more clearly the reasons for his father's incredible work ethic and his role as provider. Perino understood faithfulness to work and family: he had not missed a Saturday visit to his son Andrew in the thirty-nine years he had been living in group homes. But how could Perino have fully known how to show a father's love when his own father had not lived to model it?

Gabriel remembered something. "Dad, I heard that you accept God's invitation by opening your heart to Him above all and sealing the deal with your lips."

His father thought about it a moment and then turned to him, a twinkle in his eye, "All right. I need a pass code to heaven."

Gabriel remembered hearing Billy Graham say that his pass code to heaven was "nothing but the blood." This simplicity inspired Gabriel to offer a suggestion for his dad, "How about simply speaking the word 'Jesus' from your heart?"

Perino's countenance changed to hope. At that moment, a sudden and majestic spring rain began to fall on the desert around them. As the rain nourished new life hidden in dry ground, a renewal began within the hearts of both father and son.

Back at his home, Perino did not know that the doctors had given him only a brief time to live. Gabriel told his mother, and she agreed that it was best to just keep his sprits high and expect a miracle. Seeing her husband with much of his usual energy seemed to energize Mary, but Gabriel stayed to be with his family.

One week passed. Things were looking good. Then it happened: Perino fell out of bed and could not move his arms. After his fall, the imperialistic cancer cells waged an all-out attack on the remaining healthy tissue in his body. The family teamed with hospice care and brought in a hospital bed, oxygen machine, catheter, and morphine, but Perino's body was gradually shutting down.

Two weeks after the return home, Perino fell into a deep coma and could no longer move or speak. Gabriel did not answer his phone for anyone other than family. He moved into his parents' house and prayed by his father's side, sensing that Perino had not yet used his pass code. Gabriel expected a miracle like the one he had witnessed as a boy when his mother was near death.

He had a feeling that this miracle was going to be one of a different kind. He knew that his dad had lived a full life and that death was a part of life, but there was unfinished business in Perino's spirit. Two more weeks passed, and Perino remained in a deep coma. He was now receiving palliative care, and the family had to face several heartbreaking decisions. Then something changed.

It was a beautiful, still evening. Gabriel had taken the night shift to watch his father. He had opened both windows to create a cross breeze, but there was no air movement of any kind. In fact, it felt like the room was filled with a thick, silent fog. Kneeling at his father's bed, Gabriel read Psalm 23 aloud as a prayer. Then something inside of him made him shout "JESUS!"

Instantly, Perino bolted upright. He said, "Okay," kissed Gabriel, and then his spirit checked out of his body as he slumped back in bed. A cross breeze swelled the room for a few seconds, but the curtains billowed *out* of the window, and Gabriel realized that the breeze emanated from *inside* the room. The sense of heavy fog lifted, and the room felt as though it was filled with rays of sun. Gabriel looked down at his father's face. Perino looked like a man going on a holiday to paradise.

The pass code had worked. The healing miracle had happened; it was just a different kind of healing. The open heaven, the manifestation of heaven here and now, had healed both his mother's body and, now, his father's soul. When Gabriel realized this truth, he wept with joy. He saw that an open heaven was not just for life-and-death scenarios; it was available continually. He now had a new focus for his life search: finding the direct-access path between heaven and earth. His life search was no longer a part-time hobby. It was the main event.

As he dealt with the paperwork of his father's estate and comforted his mother, Gabriel continued to wrestle with his identity. While looking through all the documents that inventoried his father's life, he stopped and asked himself, "*What was the outcome of my own life inventory process in New York?*"

Back home with Tirzah, Gabriel found his journal, untouched since the business trip to Manhattan, and read through it. Finding no answers, he started reading Scriptures. He realized that he had carried an oversized, gold-trimmed Bible as an altar boy but had never really read it — had only revered it. He started devouring chapter after chapter until the words blurred. He fell asleep holding the book to his heart.

The Call Home

"Gabriel."

Gabriel woke with the Bible still clenched to his chest. The early dawn light silhouetted Tirzah, who was leaning over him.

"Mmh?" he responded.

"I had a dream. You need to hear it."

Gabriel set the Bible on his nightstand and sat up against his pillows, facing his wife.

Tirzah continued, "The dream was in two parts. I first saw Perino as a young man — he glowed like an angel, and he was happily getting a house ready for Mary. Then I saw you driving north from

San Diego on the freeway in thick fog. You could not read any road signs except one, which was illuminated in the fog." Tirzah paused and laid her hand on Gabriel's shoulder. "The sign read, 'Israel.'"

Israel. The word — the land, the history, everything it implied — seemed to fill Gabriel's heart.

He looked at his wife and smiled. "It looks like I am being invited to God's worldwide headquarters."

That day Gabriel started making plans to journey across the world. In the past he would have considered and analyzed such a decision for months, but this was not the past. He and Tirzah agreed that she would stay home to manage the logistics and care for the children, and he would go. He would book no tours and make no structured plans. Gabriel would wait for whatever it was that God had planned for him. He trusted that what was supposed to happen would. Three days later he was on a flight to Tel Aviv.

After seventeen hours of flight time, Gabriel arrived in Israel. He took a *sherrut*, or taxi, from the airport to the Jaffa Gate in the Old City of Jerusalem. When the van's side door opened, he was face-to-face with three Israeli Defense Forces soldiers holding automatic weapons. *This will be an interesting adventure,* Gabriel thought to himself. Thankfully, no one pointed any guns in his direction. He started walking along the stone pathway in the shadow of the Tower of David. He marveled at the ancient citadel surrounded by forty-foot-high walls. As so many before him, Gabriel felt the thrill of history beneath his feet. He found himself stopping and staring and could not wait to explore the next day. Night was falling before he settled into his guesthouse.

He woke the following morning bursting with energy, ready to conquer the Old City of Jerusalem. He enjoyed the traditional Israeli breakfast, trying to savor it while already anticipating what the day would bring. His thoughts celebrated inside his soul. *This is the Promised Land, and I have a personal invitation to be here.* Lech-L'cha! "Let's go!"

A type "A" personality, Gabriel wanted to know why he was in Israel as soon as possible. Like a frantic tourist, he turned his day into a battle plan, aiming to conquer everything in the guidebook. He attacked the first day by visiting the Temple Steps, the Western Wall, the Via Dolorosa, Gethsemane, and the Garden Tomb in a single morning. By noon his spirit, mind, and body were exhausted. He had to go back to the guesthouse and lie down. The exhaustion was more than physical; his spirit had never encountered such intense spiritual and religious conflict. Score: Jerusalem 1, Gabriel 0.

After reflection it made perfect sense that every spiritual being in the universe would be represented in the Holy Land, competing for ownership of it. The Jews, Muslims, and Christians all desired spiritual authority because the land was sacred to all three religions. Gabriel guessed that the land itself was blessed since it was the land of Jesus' birth, and the Israelites were God's chosen tribe. Looking out the window of his room across the city roofs, he gained new reverence for the land itself. He decided to let the land lead him.

From the moment Gabriel abandoned his attack of tourist sites and took time to connect with Israel's people, he realized that they consistently and cheerfully volunteered to help him learn about their land. The Israeli culture seemed to be waiting for him, and he felt encouraged to experience diversified family and business life. Since Israel's rebirth as a nation, the economy had grown approximately fifty-fold in only sixty years; that was a miracle warranting greater exploration. He was invited to visit with Jewish and Christian families in their homes and businesses. As he listened to their stories, he was drawn into their cultural mosaic. His compassion grew deeper and so did his hope to receive a life-changing revelation from this extraordinary Holy Land.

One afternoon while out walking, Gabriel approached a large gathering. Approximately three hundred Jewish teens and fifty Muslim teens had joined together for a youth conference. A few of the teens were sharing their seemingly impossible testimonies, and one eighteen-year-old Muslim girl shared a riveting story. She had battled a life-threatening illness. Without hope for her future, she volunteered to be a suicide bomber. Her friend pleaded with her to pray for a healing. She had nothing to lose, so she prayed, "Dear God who heals, heal me." That night, she was visited by someone named Yeshua Ha-Mashiach, "Jesus the Messiah," who said to her, "You are healed." The next day, the young girl's doctor confirmed that she was healed. When she finished sharing her testimony, the girl asked the Jewish teens to stand.

Weeping profusely she told them, "Not only did He heal my body, but He healed my heart. I do not hate you anymore. Please forgive me."

In the roar of applause that followed, Gabriel felt awestruck, as if he were nearing the answer to his life search. The girl's testimony was certainly a part of it, with its universal love message for all people.

As he continued to travel the countryside, Gabriel was humbled by the courage and resilience of the Jewish people in wake of the real threats they faced each and every day. Despite the struggle of life seeking life all around him, Gabriel was uncommonly relaxed. He marinated in the beauty and promise of the Holy Land. As each day passed, he grew less worried about the purpose of the trip, knowing that it would be revealed to him at the proper time.

The God of Heaven on Earth

Galilee was a beautiful homecoming. The pace and peace were the opposite of Jerusalem. Here were the rolling orchards, the green hills, the blue sea. Here, the Holy Land images came alive. Without an agenda, Gabriel was free to invest his days in a garden, meditating under the shade of an olive tree.

One afternoon, while resting near the shores of the Sea of Galilee, Gabriel heard his spirit say, *"Peace be still."* He focused on his breathing, trying to relax his body and mind. He let past hurts and future anxieties rise from his mind and be released. Then, as if following an internal, spiritual tour guide, he arrived at his heart. He heard a gentle invitation, *"Come deeper."* The pressure to climb the ladders of success evaporated in a Holy Mist, and he sensed a heaven-sent escalator lifting him. Time stood still. Luminescent, blue silk banners swayed in the breeze of his spirit. Gabriel felt as if his body and soul were being gently absorbed into the breeze. He experienced the gentle breath of life breathing him in. This soft flow of energy led him deeper and deeper, delivering him to the threshold of a door.

The door opened slowly to reveal a portal, different from anything Gabriel had known or imagined. He saw an infinite vastness beckoning him. He felt no fear, no anxiety. His spirit seemed to transcend his mind and body, and then he was traveling in the breeze. While the eyes of his heart beheld a host of images, the ears of his heart heard one phrase over and over and over again: *"Enter My Rest."*

The Awakening

On the shores of Galilee, lying under an olive tree filled with doves, approximately 7,700 miles from home, Gabriel found what he had been searching for his entire life:

Rest.

Rest past, present, and future.

Rest for all times and seasons of life.

Rest eternal. Rest internal. Rest external.

As the revelation came alive within him, Gabriel remembered a Hebrew word that a messianic rabbi had taught him: *luwn*, meaning abide or dwell and translated as rest. *But abide and rest in what?* Before Gabriel had finished the question, the answer came: *Father's Almighty love.* Gabriel had internalized the experience of John the Apostle; he had come to know and believe the love God had for him. He had seen that God *is* love. *The Father's love gives and receives rest, a rest that abides and dwells in Him at all times, a rest that manifests as a living, productive rest. If rest is a place, the address of that place is love.* Gabriel did not have to search for life outside of that love; that love was already inside of him. Gabriel was fully loved by the Father of heaven. He had just needed to acknowledge his own powerlessness in order to embrace the Father's power.

Gabriel had worked for the love of a well-meaning earthly father whose love was partly conditional and based upon work performance. Perino had not known the Father's love, and so he had not known how to show it to his son. Gabriel saw with clarity: *Restlessness is fatherlessness; rest is Father.* The symptom of restlessness in Gabriel's life had been fatherlessness. The longing of his heart — his life search — had been the reunion in oneness with Father's *unconditional* love. That love was the door to heaven on earth. The key was resting in the finished work of the Father, Son, and Spirit. As if he was meeting grace face-to-face for the first time, Gabriel was inspired to live and work differently than before.

He looked up through the olive branches and doves, symbols of peace. He saw the blue sky and smiled. The directions to the secret place were no longer secret. *An internal spiritual dwelling is real. Heaven's kingdom within is true. Heaven on earth originates* here. *Heaven on earth fulfills destiny* here. Gabriel had entered his promised land; the promise was the Cross and the land was his heart. Gabriel could now abide — could rest — in God. His life search had changed to a life search and rescue. He had been rescued from being RESTLESS for the wrong things. Gabriel was now only RESTLESS for one thing…

What would this promise look like in his personal and professional life? Could he love his wife and children with the Father's love? Could he lead business success in diverse belief environments? Suddenly, Gabriel knew that his life was an all-new work in progress: to thrive *from* the true source of rest. And he would help others do the same.

One question remained: how?

PART TWO

Personal Promised Land Playbook

Forty Years
or Forty Days?

In *The Parable of the Restless Prodigal*, we learned that we are each on an individual life search. Our life search is our path of exploration for purpose. We each have a unique life fingerprint and we will each find our purpose in a unique way. In *The Personal Promised Land Playbook*, you will identify your source and personalize your systems to find and fulfill your purpose.

Your *Personal Promised Land* is the place where your reality exceeds your wildest dreams. If you are not living those dreams, you might want to ask yourself why. The Israelites toiled for forty years to complete an estimated forty day journey. Do not make the same mistake. Your *Personal Promised Land* is a gift, but it is your job to enter and cultivate it.

The real question is *how* do we actually and practically enter and perpetually grow in our *Personal Promised Land*? The first step is to simply and profoundly recognize our power to choose our lives' purposes and outcomes. The second step is to change unproductive patterns, renew our minds, and take action.

We were designed to experience *shalom* in its full Hebraic meaning: peace, prosperity, wholeness, safety, wellness, and completeness. This is our ultimate purpose. We were designed to live from a first-place-powered, productive, rest-centric lifestyle or *Abundant Life Victory*. My passion and purpose is for you to realize your sustainable and scalable *Abundant Life Victory*.

Abundant Life Victory and the *Life Ecosystem*

Abundant Life Victory is a total quality of life based upon the dynamics of a natural ecosystem. *Abundant Life Victory* is centered on identifying our energy source, sustaining our life via that source, and then flourishing in an ever-changing environment. With that strategy in mind, I have created an innovative life technology for your *Abundant Life Victory*: the *Life Ecosystem*.

The idea of a *Life Ecosystem* is based on nature's own blueprint: an ecosystem represents order and modeling to be found in nature. Ecosystems are environments which contain communities living together in successful unity. An ecosystem can be as small as a terrarium on a third-grade classroom windowsill or as large as the Amazon Rainforest. Whatever the ecosystem's size, all of the elements within it interact to support and maintain the whole.

Natural ecosystems are powered by a main source of energy, the sun, which affects the entire environment.

Each component within an ecosystem knows its place, derives life from the whole, and sacrifices for the good of the whole. Each component has a job and knows its priorities. Your *Life Ecosystem* management will also require you to fulfill your priorities during all seasons of life.

LIFE ECOSYSTEM

Figure 4

Your unique *Life Ecosystem* will only grow as a *whole* when you grow in each *part* of your life. Your destiny is to be a well-integrated person who thrives in a well-integrated family and flourishes in a well-integrated work place. Do not settle for less than an optimal life; you were created to live a victorious life.

In the past many people thought that such victory was achieved by work/life balance. Remember the wheel of life pie charts? One slice or percentage represented your time spent at work; another slice represented time with family, etc. But what happened when you started your career/vocation? Got married? Had a child? Were promoted? Were burned out? Were unemployed? Changed careers? Had another child? Made money? Lost money? Made more money? Questioned the meaning of life? Found God? Chose a life of joy versus worry? When such changes happened, the rigid slices of the pie chart did not work.

You can have defined time goals in specific life areas. The difference is to integrate the overall authority, order, and flow in each.

Traditional time management is also obsolete. I have tested life balance and time management theories on myself and hundreds of individuals at various stages of their lives. The idea that we can balance our lives or manage our time actually causes painful frustration when we do not succeed. While tasks are important and values are vital, they must be built upon a foundation of purposeful passion within an ever-fluctuating environment.

Work/life balance and time management are myths. A *Life Ecosystem* is reality. This innovative, spirit, mind, body, biomimetic (nature-mimicking) strategy is radically changing lives. Today is the time for your *Abundant Life Victory* via your personalized *Life Ecosystem*. You can transform your life into a victorious ecosystem by optimizing your life.

Life/Work Victory

Life/Work Victory is a proven process. It is a blueprint for cultivating your *Life Ecosystem* for an *Abundant Life Victory*. Instead of chasing the failed work/life balance model, my research has led to an innovative process of dynamic optimization for each individual who is willing to accept full life accountability.

Your overall life takes precedence over your work, and balance gives way to optimization. All of your talents and dreams are honored and integrated in this comprehensive optimization process. *Life/ Work Victory* is an organic and holistic process to help you design and fulfill a better life.

One key aspect of this optimization process is the removal of life's weeds of defeat prior to planting the seeds of victory. If a gardener notices weeds in his garden, he does not snip at their leaves; he rips them out by the roots. Likewise, we start by removing the roots of any weeds preventing us from healthy growth, and *then* we sow healthy seeds.

Life/Work Victory begins with your chosen source of power. What one thing holds first place in your life and determines the outcome of all other life values? Who or what is your god/God? Who is the king of your life and where is the kingdom? Your power and purpose are in direct proportion to the power and purpose of what you put first in your life.

Whether we are cognizant of it or not, we have each chosen one thing as our master motive in life. When we live from the right motives, we win BIG, and all things become possible.

On the following pages, you will encounter the winning strategies of *Life/Work Victory*. In my extensive work with emerging talents at the university level and early career stage, I have discovered that a generation is crying out for compassionate, competent, and continual help to fill the void in these five life areas:

- *Purpose*
- *Priorities*
- *Time*
- *Goals*
- *Action*

Each of these areas has its own section. Together, this integrated Purpose/Priorities/Time/Goals/Actions toolkit will help you to live your greatest possible life. You will be led through a series of guided questions. By answering these questions with an open heart, you will activate your personalized *Life/Work Victory* process. When you learn and apply this system of freedom and discipline, you will save yourself many years of wandering in the desert of frustration. You will enter your *Personal Promised Land* ready to cultivate a life of productive rest.

Let the race begin for promises fulfilled...

Purpose

One Thing Motive

What is your purpose in life? Your meaning? Your identity? Your reason for being? Your origin and destiny? The millions of people who have read *The Purpose Driven Life* by Rick Warren have asked themselves those questions, as have the restless souls seeking solace through *Man's Search for Meaning* by Viktor Frankl.

Your purpose may be honor, morals, health, family, work, titles, money, power, addictions, or a higher purpose. We all look at life through the life lens of our purpose, our "one thing." That one thing is your primary motivating factor. It dictates your attitudes and behavior in every area of life. To cultivate a productive *Life Ecosystem*, you need to know your source — the who or what that provides energy and power for all components of your life. This decision is personal; it is subjective for each individual person. This choice empowers your *One Thing Motive*. A *One Thing Motive* is the primary driver that causes you to act or behave in a certain way.

Prior to revealing the *how* systems, I'd like to focus on the *who*, *why*, and *what* foundations of success. I struggled while writing this section of the book because of the diversity of people whom I serve. I serve friends who are seeking a better life, and I serve businesses that are seeking more success. I also have business friends seeking spiritual empowerment and spiritual friends seeking business empowerment.

My solution is to stay focused on a common denominator: seeking the best in each person. I see the hidden fire of promise in each individual and business. My gift is a process to fan those flames and release people into their greatest victory by helping them to embrace accountability for their own decisions, actions, and results.

Parts Two and Three of this book offer simple processes and tools of success known as *Optimizers*. These are proven, customizable *Optimizers* for life and work breakthroughs.

Before we arrive at our personal and professional *Optimizers*, we must address purpose. Our purpose is our source. Purpose precedes life and work systems. Find your source of power, and you will find your purpose. In Part One, Gabriel discovered the power of restful productivity. How do we to do the same?

We start by defining "rest" as a lifestyle of restful productivity. Let me give you an example. While a friend and I were paddle boarding on the lake, we spotted a bald eagle in a tree. As we watched, the eagle lifted off from the tree branch, gracefully glided on the wind toward the water, and pulled a fish from the lake. I was astounded at the eagle's effortless way of *receiving* his reward. He was not flustered or anxious. He was not second-guessing. He identified his goal, and then he went for it.

Do you know why I wrote a book entitled *Restless?* I was restless for most of my life, and that restlessness led me to seek peace, to seek contentment, to seek rest. I found rest in God. Now, He is my purpose. He is my source. He is my system. I had to start from that place of purpose to move into my *Personal Promised Land.* Since making that decision, I am experiencing far more of the eagle's version of reward. Rest in my own spirit led to rest in my own skin. You will have the opportunity to personalize your purpose, source, and system.

It is worth saying again: purpose precedes personal and professional victory. To set you up for your own victory, I would like to share the foundational system, the *7Rs of Rest.*

The

*R*s

of Rest

Revelation

Relative

Relationship

Responsibility

Results

Renewal

Rewards

As our first set of *Optimizers,* the *7Rs of Rest* are processes and tools designed to help us define our purpose. After an introduction to each "R" based upon my personal experience, you will be asked to write your own, customized version.

REVELATION

What is our life's purpose? Is there an answer — a truth — a revelation — that towers above all others?

Such questions will always stir great debate, but I have found that debate alone will not produce breakthrough. Personal exploration will. Personal encounter will. Personal revelation will. The answers were revealed to me by falling in love with God. Perfect and complete love is possible.

Bill Johnson, a global change leader and Senior Pastor at Bethel Church summarized it by saying, "One of the greatest tragedies of our time is that the Bible was interpreted by people who were not in love [with God])."[4]

For years I outsourced my intimacy with God to others. Not anymore. This Almighty love revelation is only gained in an intimate, first-person experience. I am receiving revelatory sight by falling in love with God. By revealing myself to Him, He reveals Himself to me. As this process unfolds, revelation orchestrates the reason and rhythm for my life. Now it is your turn.

How do I receive life-guiding revelation? Do I know truth when I hear it?

....

....

....

....

....

....

....

....

....

....

RELATIVE

Who am I? Whose physical and spiritual DNA do I carry? What is the complete story of the code in me? What is my true identity?

Our perceived and desired image is related to that of another. I have found my identity as a child of God. The eternal adoption invitation is imprinted on my heart. Here, now, and forever, we all have access to this abundant life birthright as the everlasting Father's son or daughter. To see myself as he sees me is my heart's desire.

Who is my ultimate role model? What is my desired image of myself?

....

....

....

....

....

....

....

....

....

....

RELATIONSHIP

How can I really know Him as a loving Father? A protector? A provider? A friend? A teacher? A counselor? A business partner?

Time, energy and focus are the currency of a solid and growing relationship. The more we spend time listening to God, the more we hear Him. Two-way, real-time communication with God is not only possible, it's life-changing. I invest in this relationship and discover a hidden place within that drives my external world; life becomes a beautiful, multi-dimensional journey.

How do I build a relationship with my ultimate role model? How do I infuse that relationship into myself and others?

....

....

....

....

....

....

....

....

....

....

RESPONSIBILITY

As a child of God, how do I fully honor my Father's reputation and resources?

The grace of being born into this position is free. Harvesting the fullness of the finished work is not. As an heir to the King of Glory, I am held to a higher standard. This accountability requires taking risks and persevering. I seek to use my talents to honor all levels of family in my life.

Revelation requires responsibility. At times, our revelation exceeds our obedience to follow through. Responsibility requires obedience.

In fact, the Hebrew word for "hearing" is *Shema*, meaning to both *hear and obey*.

Responsibility comes from the Father's love, not for it.

How do I define my responsibility to maximize my heritage and talents? What risks am I willing to take to do so?

....

....

....

....

....

....

....

....

....

RESULTS

How do I define success? How does my life-purpose influence my priorities and goals? How do I measure my progress?

Above all, my focus is to build a thriving relationship with my Father. From that relationship, I diligently listen for anointed assignments. When I work through those assignments — which often look like pragmatic life and work experiences — I humbly yet boldly advance as a son and a partner in the family business. As I do, my eternal apprenticeship continues to gain momentum in unimaginable, big-picture, and long-term ways.

How do I define success? What process do I use to make decisions and set priorities?

....

....

....

....

....

....

....

....

....

RENEWAL

How will I stay refreshed amid trials *and* triumphs? How do I stay focused on my purpose and win this race of life?

A lifestyle rooted in *Teshuvah* (a Hebrew word meaning repentance or a changed life) is a key ingredient in the life-success recipe. Every day, I have a fresh opportunities to learn, to grow, and to be changed. Adversity can be transformed into advancement. I embrace the continual stretching, because I know it will help me to fulfill my destiny. Instead of entering the Promised Land before I am ready to steward it, I will be ready for greater responsibility.

How do I continually renew my heart and mind? What can I do to better overcome trials?

....

....

....

....

....

....

REWARDS

Rest is my best reward from the Father. From this abiding place, I receive His Almighty power and love in the form of strength, courage and joy. This is good news that gets better; the more I seek to store up treasures in heaven, the more they are manifested both on earth and beyond.

How do I receive heaven's rewards? What can I do to increase my knowledge and enjoyment of all of the rewards that are available to me?

....

....

....

....

....

To summarize: my purpose-discovery process led me to my *One Thing:* an all-powerful desire to channel the fire that burns within me. This discovery then led me to the living source of Almighty power and love, which intensified my purpose to make a difference. The purpose *of* life produces purpose *in* life. They are proportional to one another. My personal *One Thing Motive* is God. I abide in the highest form of love from heaven for life on earth.

Purpose changes your life. I can personally relate to William Wilberforce's discovery. He had led a purposeless life until he discovered his God and a purpose greater than himself. In his personal diary, he wrote, "I am wretched, and miserable, and blind, and naked. What infinite love, that Christ should die to save such a sinner [as me]."[4] And yet Wilberforce's co-laboring with God led to one of the greatest moves of freedom that the world has ever known: the abolition of slavery in Britain.

When you implement the *One Thing Motive,* you will see new movement and momentum in your life. This first step covers your purpose, your meaning, your identity, your truth, your god/God, and your success. Your response will define and influence all areas of your life, so it is important that you craft it carefully. Identify the *One Thing Motive* that will be the ultimate purpose for all of your actions.

My One Thing Motive *is:*

Your *One Thing Motive* will also define the roles you play in life
and work. Now you are going to define those life/work roles. They
can include both *being* roles and *doing* roles. *Being* roles might look
like:

- *"I am a peaceful person."*
- *"I am a restless person."*
- *"I am a creative person."*
- *"I am an analytical person."*
- *"I am a joyful person."*
- *"I am an anxious person."*
- *"I am a fully alive person."*

And *doing* roles might look like:

- *"I am a son/daughter."*
- *"I am a mother/father."*
- *"I am a flight attendant.*
- *"I am a vice president."*
- *"I am an artist and writer."*
- *"I am a marathon runner."*
- *"I am a loving friend."*

Add as many *being* and *doing* roles as you want, including those
you have in careers, hobbies, and passions. By the way, your *being*
passions and talents can and will transform your *doing* if you let
identity lead action. It is not only *what* you do but *why* and *how*

you do it that counts. Begin each role with I am a/an. If you need more room, keep going.

My Life/Work Roles

I am a/an ....

I am a/an ....

I am a/an ....

I am a/an ....

I am a/an ....

I am a/an ....

I am a/an ....

SWOT

Albert S. Humphrey, an American business and management consultant, created the acronym SWOT as a business tool for strategic planning. It also works for personal planning. The SWOT framework will help you to maximize your strengths and minimize your weaknesses. SWOT is composed of:

Strengths

Weaknesses

Opportunities

Threats

Strengths and weaknesses are internal factors; opportunities and threats are external factors. Knowing how all of these apply to you is essential for optimizing your life.

STRENGTHS

What are you good at? Great at? Your goal is to make sure you are leveraging your talents in a systematic way, while remembering that you can continually build upon those talents. Personality tests like the Myers-Briggs Type Indicator (MBTI®) can be helpful in discovering your strengths. For example, my tests identify my strengths as a protector and builder. List your greatest talents and achievements.

My strengths are:

....

....

....

....

....

....

....

....

....

....

WEAKNESSES

We're generally quite aware of our weaknesses. We just are not always honest with ourselves that we have them. Once you face your weaknesses, you can manage them. List your greatest weaknesses and failures.

My weaknesses are:

....

....

....

....

....

....

....

....

....

....

....

....

John Maxwell, a preeminent author and leader of leaders, talks about "failing forward." This is a methodology for using failures as stepping stones. If well-managed, missteps transform into stair steps. We turn our past mistakes into future victories. To do so, we have to be aware of failure factors – that is any weakness that increases our likelihood of tripping up. I like to detect personal landmines and devise a counterattack strategy that I can implement when I see myself stepping into my weaknesses. For example, I have developed a simple acronym that reminds me to take time out for rapid response management of my primary weaknesses. PAUSE identifies my weaknesses and helps me to proactively manage them:

Procrastination

Anger

Ubiquitous

Speeding

Exhaustion

PAUSE also provides thought programming and an alternative action for me to follow:

Procrastination — When procrastinating due to perfectionism or mental paralysis, I do just the opposite and take immediate action.

Anger — When experiencing anger, I take a breath, take a mental timeout, bridle my tongue, and wait twenty-four hours (if possible).

Ubiquitous — When trying to be all things to all people, I remember to focus on my power source, my *One Thing Motive*. This helps me reestablish my essential priorities.

Speeding — When pressing life's pedal to the metal (having received many speeding tickets in my lifetime, I am an expert on this subject), I simply breathe, slow down, and pace myself.

Exhaustion — When I first recognize the symptoms of exhaustion, I watch what I say so that I do not put my foot in my mouth. I then revisit my weekly plan to make real-time changes that will optimize my energy.

Consider creating your own acronym for your primary weaknesses. Include an alternative action plan so that your strengths lead to a better choice than your weaknesses would.

OPPORTUNITIES

Opportunities are simply situations that favor your purpose. But there is an opportunity cost for selecting one course of action over another — every choice means not choosing something else. When we know who we are and what we want, we will gain opportunistic eyes for the infinite possibilities before us. Seeing new opportunities begins with being grateful for our current opportunities. What current opportunities are you grateful for? The very act of writing them down often reveals even more. Each day is rich in new opportunities; which ones do you see?

My opportunities are:

....

....

....

....

....

....

....

....

....

....

....

....

You have the opportunity to live a productive, restful life. To do so, you first take the opportunity to remove obstacles — weeds — that are preventing your growth (some of those may be your threats, see below). Then you can step into opportunities for personal growth, health, relationships, and career.

THREATS

Threats to our *Abundant Life Victory* can be so embedded in our lives that we do not even recognize them as threats. To root out long-standing threats, I scheduled a SOZO session, (Spirit-led, interactive, inner healing) at Bethel Church in Redding, California. *Sozo* is a Greek word meaning "saved, healed, delivered, and set free." Inner healing helped me conquer generational/cultural lies, lack of forgiveness, wrongful beliefs and ties to the past so that I could move forward. You may want to take time and seek assistance to identify any lies you are believing about yourself so that you can be set free. Spiritual/mental health issues are rampant in our society and are often swept under the carpet. To overcome deep-seated issues, I encourage you to seek additional help (trusted friend, mentor, therapy, physician, etc.)

A key to mobilizing your forward momentum is to "get over

yourself and get moving," as my powerful and lovely wife, Linda, says. Just as a business entering a new market will carefully examine the barriers to its entry, we must consider barriers to our *Personal Promised Land.* The biggest and most dangerous barriers to entry are personal pride and a closed heart or mind.

Years ago, I injured my ankle playing sports. It partially healed, but whenever I was running, the restricted movement let me know that something was still wrong. I realized it was time to suck it up and go for the root-cause solution. I scheduled an appointment for bodywork to break up the scar tissue and restore mobility. The first session was incredibly painful, but I had to embrace the pain for new freedom.

I learned my lesson: if I try to move forward into my destiny without healing old injuries, those injuries will continue to hinder my progress. Sometimes we need help in the healing process. It is okay if you have to take that proverbial step back before you step forward. Perhaps it is time to forgive yourself or someone else. What keeps you from moving forward?

My threats are:

....

....

....

....

....

....

....

....

....

....

....

....

Life/Work Tests

24-Hour Open Day

If you had only twenty-four hours to live, how would you prioritize your time and energy? If you could do anything you wanted, what would you do? Run to your church? Hold your child closely? Call your mom? Finish your game of tennis? Empty your e-mail in-box? Take a nap? What would you do?

If I had twenty-four hours left to live and could do anything I wanted, I would:

....

....

....

....

....

....

....

....

....

....

24-Hour Structured Day

Perhaps the more important question than *what* you would do is *how* you would do it. So now you get to answer this question as if you were the only one who knew this was your last day on earth. If you had to go to work, take care of the kids, keep your appointments — whatever is currently on your calendar for the next twenty-four hours — if you had do all of it with the *secret* knowledge that this would be your last day, what would you do and how would you do it?

If I had twenty-four hours left to live my structured day and I was the only one who knew this, I would:

....

....

....

....

....

....

....

....

....

....

....

This exercise is a reminder that we are to live each day fully alive: not just the weekend; not just the day at the beach; not just the wedding, or the retirement party. In fact, if you can not live today fully alive, you will not be able to enjoy any of those days to their fullest.

Your Epitaph

Even if you do not plan on having a graveyard burial, imagine that you have chosen your grave plot and selected your tombstone. You met with the stone engraver and he gave you a limit of 140 characters or fewer for your epitaph. What short message would summarize your legacy?

Figure 5

My epitaph would read:

Life/Work Leading Indicators

Now imagine you are back in grade school. It is Saturday and you have done all of your chores. You have the whole day to do whatever you want. What do you — *did* you — do? We can learn a lot about what fulfills us by looking from our adulthoods back to our childhoods.

As a child, I felt most fulfilled when I:

....

....

....

....

....

....

....

....

Now think of life, education, and work experiences that have provided you with the greatest fulfillment as an adult.

*As an adult, I feel most fulfilled in **life** when I:*

....

....

....

....

....

....

....

....

....

....

....

....

....

....

....

....

*As an adult, I feel most fulfilled at **work** when I:*

....

....

....

....

....

....

....

....

....

....

....

Look back at what you have written. Are there any overlaps between your childhood sense of fulfillment and your adult life/work fulfillment? Pay attention to those. Are there very few overlaps? Is there a facet of fulfillment from childhood that you have left behind?

Let's identify opportunities for growth related to your sense of fulfillment. Keep in mind that fulfillment is not so much a matter of *what* we do but *how* we do it. How do we recapture our childlike joy in life? Dream for a moment.

I want to recapture the joy of my childhood in adulthood by:

Sometimes, in the process of growing up, we grow out of our childfullness. Remaining childlike is essential to remaining full of wonder, joy, and anticipation — all traits necessary for creative problem solving, relationships, and overall fulfillment in life. Your purpose, your *One Thing Motive,* can help to remind you of your heart's desires.

Priorities

Ranking Priorities

As I mentioned earlier, we are moving beyond the concept of life/work balance and into a more realistic and integrated *Life Ecosystem*. Your personal ecosystem will shift with the inevitable changing seasons and intangibles of life.

In nature, the sun is the energy source for an ecosystem. Through photosynthesis, plants create food by converting sunlight into energy. In your *Life Ecosystem*, whatever you put first — that one thing — becomes the energy source for every component of your life, and all of those components must work together in harmony for your ecosystem to flourish. That harmony is the result of implementing a proven system. I have successfully taught these simple yet profound steps to team members of many organizations. Throughout this section, you will find testimonials from my past and present team members who use this system. These people have seen incredible breakthroughs in their lives when they have implemented our second set of *Optimizers*, the *7Fs of Freedom*.

The *F*s of Freedom

Faith

Fitness

Family

Future

Finances

Friends

Fun

FAITH

Figure 6

FAITH

Faith is the opposite of fear. Fear is the root cause of anxiety; faith empowers the restful productivity that creates a life of anxiety-free living. Communications Pathologist Dr. Caroline Leaf writes that, "Faith and fear are not just emotions, but spiritual forces with chemical and electrical representation in the body."[6] Faith walks hand in hand with purpose. What do you put your faith in above all else? Who or what is your god/God? This can be seen with Bjorn:

> *During the last few years, I learned to live and work from faith. I entered a work arena where I had no experience. I wanted to be given a chance. I had to humble myself and I'd say, "Lord, I do not know what to do. I need you to help me." When I surrendered myself and lived in faith, I found that I had the ability to succeed. Those I worked for and with believed in me as well. I came away with tremendous confidence. That healthy environment changed me.*
>
> *The skills I learned through this process have made me realize that for an Abundant Life Victory, each of the 7Fs must be*

valued. For me, these tools have opened up an entire new world filled with amazing opportunities.

I always knew that I wanted to live in Asia; I was just waiting for the right time. I took an incredible leap of faith, quit my job, and bought a one-way ticket to Taiwan. Within the first month I had not one but two jobs. I am living my dream!

— BJORN

Figure 7

FITNESS

Fitness here means the total integration of your spirit, mind, and body in harmony. I used to try compartmentalizing these aspects of fitness; it did not work. The divine order of the body begins with spirit, then soul (mind, emotions, will), then body. You are one entity. Your spirit is the vice president, your mind the director, and your body the manager.

I have conducted extensive experiments in this arena and learned that there are three candidates running for the presidential office of my spirit-mind-body: Holy Spirit (all-powerful, loving, spontaneous, inviting); my mind (analyzing, controlling, judgmental); and competing spirits (fear, uncertainty, doubt). The great thing about recognizing the competition is that you can choose whom to listen to. And, even if you have been listening to the wrong voice, you can reprogram your mind, emotions, and will. Your spirit will be directed by the president of your choice.

So many people have good intentions for fitness, yet they struggle for meaningful and lasting change. We must see fitness in the completeness that it is:

> *To understand how spirit, mind, and body work together starts with understanding the reality that the three are already integrated, and that they follow a hierarchy. The spirit leads the mind and body. When it does not, we'll be unhealthy. The practices in the Life/Work Victory process are practical and necessary. They expose people to things they know but never think about. They make it painfully obvious where we're falling short, but that it's fully in our capability to make our lives the way we want. It's like a game. I play to win.*
>
> — DENNIS

Figure 8

FAMILY

When I look at old photos and scan the faces, I realize that many of those smiling people are now strangers to me.

I recently asked myself, "Of all of these wonderful people I have met, who is still actively involved in my life?" With the exception of some amazing friends who transcend friendship, the resounding answer is: my wife, children, siblings, and parents. In other words: my family.

What constitutes a family? Unconditional love, forgiveness, acceptance, encouragement, brutal honesty, gentle humility. What a blessing to be surrounded by the gift of people who usually love me, occasionally hate me, but who stick with me no matter what. Whether by birth or by divine gift, I can count on family:

Experiencing Life/Work Victory has made me realize there is more to being in a family than just showing up. It's easy to get caught up in the day-to-day stuff: how to make ends meet, how to pay your bills, how to get through all the stuff that comes up during the day. Add on work with its own set

95

of responsibilities, and it can become overwhelming. I have learned how important it is to organize and manage my time, set priorities and take care of myself. When I do these things, I am actively managing my life. I can then spend time with my husband and family and give them what they need and not feel that anyone is being shortchanged. My husband, Tim, and I consistently reevaluate our priorities to maintain a flourishing life ecosystem.

— BREANNE

My experience with the Life/Work Victory process has given me the confidence to ask for things instead of waiting for them to be offered and to drive my future — not sit back and wait for it to happen. This assertiveness has empowered me in many areas of my life. Like taking the leap and asking Jessi (now my wife) out for the first time — not just waiting, hoping it would happen. When I met Jessi, I was a student, and we were both working at a local coffee house. She thought I was sort of a goofball. I thought she was gorgeous. I did not think I had a chance. The assertiveness and confidence I have gained allowed me to do things I would not normally do — things that could impact my future, like dating Jessi or buying my first rental property.

I had been saving and knew that I wanted to invest in real estate. I found a property I liked, but, due to market conditions, I had a very short time to make my decision. Through prayer and belief in my decision-making ability, I moved forward. Jessi and I are now happily married and on our way to owning additional properties. We are planning for our future and are taking steps to make our dreams our realities.

— JAMES

Figure 9

FUTURE

By future, I am referring to a career or a vocation. Vocation, or calling, is the place where our talents reach their full expression. In my mentoring workshops and sessions, I see people focusing overwhelmingly on their careers and callings. Work *is* vital for our sustenance and our joy. We were made to enjoy work. It is a wonderful feeling to stand back and enjoy closing a big deal, engineering an algorithm, or designing a house. The challenge is that sometimes we let our work become toil (overanxious, unenjoyable labor), and we sacrifice the other components of the *7F* system. There are seasons when this is necessary, but after these seasons, the ecosystem must be brought back into harmony for an *Abundant Life Victory*. (In the next part of the book, we will explore how to cultivate the highest levels of enjoyment and productivity at work.):

> *Dream big: this is my special juice in life. My message. My hope. My gift. Before I experienced Life/Work Victory, I was sure that my dream was to be a hardworking, significant businesswoman, period. I thought I knew it all. Little did I know that there was much more to life than simply being a*

hard worker. The 7Fs of Freedom are not just about succeeding at work but about embracing a free life in all areas. You see, freedom is discipline in all areas of life working together. I have learned the painful yet fruitful lesson that freedom demands a higher standard of living. Rick and I coined the phrase, "dream shock." It means going all out for your dreams knowing that they will both take and give everything. Peace be with you on your dream journey.

— ANA

Through Life/Work Victory training, I have learned the power of asking "what if?" What if you worked in an environment that was linked to your overall life success? What if you were mentored beyond just doing a job and into the vision alignment of why you worked in the first place? What if the one thing that is most important in your life became the fuel for every part of your life? For me, the "what if?" journey changed my life. After two years of financial challenges I became the top wage earner on my team. The momentum continued to build. I met my favorite adventurer, Bear Grylls, and went on my first tropical vacation, scuba diving in crystal-clear water. I saw my first major league baseball game with box tickets that were a gift. I lost 20 pounds, reached my goal weight, and gained more energy than I have ever had. By taking ownership of the Life/Work Victory training, I finally learned what it takes to move from a fear-filled lifestyle into a faith-led lifestyle of success.

— SIMEON

Figure 10

FINANCES

Let's face it, money is important. Finances involve both stewardship and growth. Money should be your employee, not your boss. Many people let money call the shots. Recently, I watched a *Saturday Night Live* skit about the credit crisis. Steve Martin, the guest, was introduced to a revolutionary wealth program. Shocked, he replied with something like, "You mean I do not spend money that I do not have?" Yes! Understanding simple principles such as the "latte effect," how cutting back on the little things can add up over time, can make a big difference to your budget. In the upcoming section on goals, you will find references to proven, practical, and spiritual financial systems that will help you become victorious with your finances:

> *We've been able to do amazing things. We wanted to be debt free. The Life/Work Victory process was great; the fundamental building blocks helped us to create a financial structure. We meet regularly. We are on the same page. We have set a strict budget, and we know what our goals are. We have a certain amount of money for spending, for food, for fun. Communicating on a weekly, monthly, and annual basis has helped us with our*

finances. We have a clear plan. Our first step was getting $1K in the bank, second was getting our college debt paid. There's clear communication. We were successful in paying off all of our debts and were able to take our dream trip to Israel — the trip paid for in full, in advance. Financial success has helped us focus more energy on our relationship. We know we are doing this part of our life really well!

— TIM and CANDESS

FRIENDS

Figure 11

FRIENDS

Friends are one of our greatest joys in life, especially friendships that are true, loving, and lasting. Whom can you be yourself with? Whom do you enjoy walking with, traveling with, or playing with? Who is there for you no matter what? These are the friends you see off-screen, the friends who sit at your dining room table. A wide variety of acquaintances and networks are wonderful; today, both real and virtual connections are vital. But keep face-to-face time as an integral part of your definition of friendship:

As I get older, I realize the importance of relationships and the value of friendships. I have a buddy I met when I was five who is still one of my closest friends. Through building strong relationships, I want to help people feel important and create opportunities for them. I want to be the best at encouraging and loving others. I want to improve myself and those around me so that we can continue to help others. (Sal)

I want to build a community and pursue relationships instead of waiting for them to come to me. In my work environment I've learned a lot about grace, giving people room to grow, and letting them learn, because that was given to me. It is definitely a family dynamic. It's not as scary to confront; it's safe. I am learning to be more confident in who I am and to communicate with greater precision and power in all situations. (Haddie)

— SAL and HADDIE

Figure 12

FUN

We all know what fun is, but not all of us maintain childlike joy and wonder throughout our lives. Remember what it was like at recess to simply run out of the classroom and shriek with joy at the sheer thought of play? We are still children at heart. I forgot that for a season of my life, and now I am so thankful to have remembered it. Fun is necessary. Consistently having fun and being joyful will help us keep it together when things seem to be falling apart. What makes you lose track of time? What makes you smile and laugh? Do those things. Fun will add life to your years and years to your life:

> *As I have participated in the Life/Work Victory classes, I have learned that freedom begets order, and order begets freedom. The more order in your daily schedule/daily life, the more freedom you have to do what you enjoy most. When you take care of the requirements, you have the time and resources to do the fun things that bring you joy! Your joy helps you to be the best you can be in all areas of your life. If you are not in your joy, you are not in your strength. One of the things I love is salsa*

dancing. I've been having great fun dancing, meeting with choreographers and learning every dance move I can. I have also begun travelling with salsa — going to salsa conferences, workshops, and competitions. The surprise was that Life/Work Victory has fun benefits!

— ERICA

These are the *7Fs of Freedom*. All seven of these components need to be optimized for your *Life Ecosystem* to be fruitful. As I am sure you have experienced, there are seasons when your ecosystem has to adapt to various changes and "weather conditions." There are times in life where *managed* imbalance is imperative. If you experience an extreme family change, you will probably rearrange priorities linked to your future and take time off of work. If you suddenly make or lose a large sum of money, other components will shift accordingly. At any given time, one life component will be subordinate to another.

The idea of a *Life Ecosystem* is biomimetic: it mimics nature. When we look out our windows at different times of the day or year, we see fluctuation. The image of a continually growing and changing *Life Ecosystem* frees us from thinking that every area of our lives must be in perfect balance like some cosmic scale. When we prioritize our lives with an ecosystem in mind, we will operate at our highest capacities.

A recent workshop attendee was unsure about how to move beyond a failed pattern of priority setting. I told him: "If you truly desire freedom and are failing in the status quo, you have one option: change!" It took me many years to know my absolute priority in life and then to harmonize my relative priorities. For example, for years my family was my second priority until I realized that I was not much good to them when I was constantly exhausted. I shifted my Fitness (spirit-mind-body) to number two in my *7Fs*, and my family prospered. The order of the *Life Ecosystem* is vital to its overall health. Family is a priority over work, yet work helps to provide for my family. You can invest a lot of yourself in work and also invest quality and quantity time into your family members: they are your legacy. As I review my life and all my work achievements, I can say that the greater adventure is my wife, Linda, and our children.

Here is an example of what your *Life Ecosystem* can look like:

Figure 13

Now you will prioritize your *7Fs of Freedom.* I relisted the *7Fs* below at random; choose which one of the seven will take first place in your life and in what order the others will follow.

Fill in the *7Fs* in the order of priority you want them to have in your life:

**Family, Future (Work), Faith,
Fitness (Spirit, Mind, Body), Fun, Finances, Friends**

1. _____   2. _____

3. _____   4. _____

5. _____   6. _____

7. _____

Your *Abundant Life Victory*

At this point, I hope that you are beginning to picture how your *Life Ecosystem* can flourish. What does *Abundant Life Victory* look like? Take a moment, close your eyes, and picture it. What images, feelings, circumstances, and relationships do you see? Paint a picture in words and/or images of your ideal, fully functioning ecosystem. Be sure to include your *One Thing Motive* and each of the *7Fs of Freedom*. Use more pages if necessary.

My Abundant Life Victory looks like:

....

....

....

....

....

....

RESTLESS

Time

_____

Great168

Now that we have identified our priorities, we have to manage them. Time is simply a tool with which to organize priorities. We lead our lives by taking dominion over our time, which protects us from the law of diminishing returns (continually doing more while getting less done). Rest and restoration are vital.

To begin, the *Optimizers* that represent the *5Ps of Perspective* help us to lead our thoughts. To make your priorities sustainable, you need to be:

Perpetual — Know the difference/link between temporal and eternal life.

Panoramic — Adopt a broad-based, *mosaic* view of your situation.

Paradox-less — Embrace great truths that have seemingly contradictory positions that are complementary (e.g. Freedom = Discipline, Trials = Triumph, Heaven on Earth = Joy and

Suffering.)

Process — Remember that you are a continual work in process.

Present — Stay present in the beauty and wonder of each moment.

We all have 168 hours per week to live life to the fullest. I call this the *Great168* because our personal greatness is directly proportional to the way we manage our time and energy. At the beginning of each week, visualize an hourglass filled with these precious 168 hours. That's 10,080 minutes, or 648,000 seconds. How will yours be used? Currently, I am testing a 7Fs ordered and flowing plan that includes 50 hours work time, 50 hours sleep time, 20 hours single-task God time, 20 hours family/recreation time, and 28 hours open, flexible time. I like to learn from the Hebrew calendar where the new day begins the previous night.

This *Great168* is an ongoing, disciplined process. It is vital to harvest the infinite blessings in your life. The following chart shows the main areas of life you inhabit over the course of a week. In the first blank column, write the number of hours you currently spend in each area. In the second blank column, write the number of hours you desire to spend in each area.

THE GREAT 168

Life Areas	Current Hours	Desired Hours
Work/Professional Development		
Sleep		
Family		
Recreation		
Spiritual		
Friends		
Money Management		
Mind/Thought Management		
Body Health Management		
Internet/T.V. (non Work)		
Other		
Other		

Figure 14

Do you see any disparities between where your time is currently being spent and where you would like it to be spent? What changes can you make to improve your use of time?

Time Orchestration Tools

If, like almost everyone, you have a few areas you would like to improve, consider the following time orchestration tools:

Life Area Integration — Realize that there will be overlaps among life areas when inevitable life-area multitasking occurs.

Priorities/Power Zones — Use the Pareto Principle (also known as the 80/20 Rule) for your schedule: potentially, 80 percent of the value of your effort is derived from 20 percent of the relative time investment. Also know, respect, and plan for when your energy is highest and lowest.

Time Margins/Spirit Standard Time — Build buffer zones into your schedule. I am learning to operate in what I call Spirit Standard Time. When we are truly one with the Spirit, we operate in a different dimension — the time zone of restful productivity.

Time Multipliers/Dividers — Invest more time with people who multiply energy and less time with people who divide energy.

Delegation — Understand the principle of core competency and orchestrating resources for optimal productivity. Do what you do best and let others do what they do best. When you maximize your strengths and let others maximize theirs, everyone succeeds.

The power of YES & NO — Honor your yes, and say no more often to those things that rob from your yes.

Personal Reward System — Add play to work by preparing a simple reward system. A reward system will help you to do the things that you do not like to do but that are essential to your long-term success. For every block of time you work, plan a reward for yourself: a walk, a vitamin drink, coffee with friends, etc. After finishing big projects, reward yourself with larger things as you are able: (e.g. a special dinner out with friends, a weekend away.) Reward yourself, both during the process and when you have finished the project.

3Ds of Daily Excellence

Figure 15

Now that you know where and how you want your time to be spent, you can prepare your daily schedule and weekly calendar. For me, each day starts with the *3Ds of Daily Excellence* that integrate the mosaic dimensions of my life:

Delight — Know the Lord through worship, prayer, meditation and work.

Declarations — Speak new life over personal landmines and program your thoughts.

Duties — Confirm and commit to your "A" priorities for the day.

A fine line exists between a heart-led, fluid process and a strict ritual. The *3Ds* form a heart-led, fluid process that keeps me focused. To keep them fresh, I vary the activities, similar to cross training. My practice of the *3Ds of Daily Excellence* is a direct result of my commitment to live a practical *and* Spirit-led life of complete victory in all dimensions of my life. God is Spirit, and I connect with Him via His Holy Spirit who resides in my spirit. My spirit directs my soul (mind-emotions-will), which in turn directs my body. I start every morning by consciously connecting to the source of my power (God). This power leads me through my day in victory.

What do these *3Ds* look like on my weekly calendar? I break every day down into three power zones:

POWER ZONE 1

Personal Devotions — In my effort to start each day with the *3Ds of Daily Excellence*, God receives the first fruits and focus of each new day. Within the first moments of waking, I practice **Delight** and **Declarations**. These continue throughout the day, as I move on to **Duties** like...

Physical Exercise — Exercise of your choice. Honor your temple and your temple will honor you.

Mental Exercise — 360-degree thinking helps you to overcome yourself and do the opposite of procrastination. 360-degree thinking is taking control of negative thoughts and turning them into positive and thankful thoughts.

POWER ZONE 2

"A" Priorities — These are the key priorities to focus on in the first half of the day. The "A" priorities are documented on a daily priority list and actively managed.

"B" Priorities & Relationship Management — These actions come in the second half of the day and are also managed in a systematic manner.

POWER ZONE 3

Evening Family/Recreation — The day's work is done. It is time for family, community, play, etc.

Wind Down — This is the time when the plane is approaching the runway to land for the day and spend the night in the hangar. I have an active mind, and I have to relax/reposition my thinking before bed. It helps me to write down unfinished business and ideas for the next day.

For me, the *3Ds of Daily Excellence* are imperative!

Of course, you are fully empowered to customize your priorities to fit your beliefs and lifestyle. There are plenty of tools to do so: day planners, color-coded online calendars, etc. In addition, you may find it helpful to schedule simple yet vital activities like hydration, nutrition, and quick periods to rest your eyes and move your body, especially if your work involves a lot of sitting. If you do sit at a desk all day, office ergonomics are vital to maintain your health and productivity.

Sabbath

I also invest special Sabbath time once a week. This is a dedicated time to honor God and reset my life. This time is not set aside because of obedience to the law but from a desire to remain centered. A weekly Sabbath will actually multiply my productivity the following week. Without it, I become like a chicken with my head cut off, running around with no purpose. Sabbath is a time for re-centering.

Sabbath may be a time of laughing, crying, singing, dancing, walking, hiking, etc. For me, it sometimes needs to become a business meeting with God so that I can adjust areas of my life in order to release rest.

God loves it when you go deeper into your oneness with Him through specificity, intensity, and time. Practice the art of being still and streaming rest and spontaneity. Doing so will make you more creative and multiply your productivity. How long can you go without a freeway of thoughts speeding through your mind? Practice stillness in whatever way works for you. When you do, you will replenish the wellspring of your spirit.

Refresh365

Each day in a 365-day year presents you with the gift of a new beginning. God's tender mercies are fresh each day. Whatever has happened in the past, whatever is happening soon, choose to start each day with a clean slate.

Live the *Great168* and *Refresh365* from a place of healthy perspective, new beginnings, and restful productivity.

Goals

Goals/Plans/Resources (GPR)

Goals are dreams that jump out of bed each day and go to work! Each of us is created for greatness; but often, somewhere along the way to greatness, we conform our goals to a world system, and our dreams get lost. We will benefit the world more by being ourselves and rising to become whom we were created to be.

Each exercise in this section has been geared toward helping you articulate and activate your *Abundant Life Victory*. You have already defined your purpose, priorities and time. Now it is time to activate them. Goals are life-purpose enablers. This section helps you set goals, which are accompanied by proven plans and resources.

Let's return to the *7Fs of Freedom* for our goal-setting framework. Remember that each goal is sourced from what holds first place in your life — in your one thing. With your *One Thing Motive* in first place, you will identify your *Goals/Plans/Resources* in this section, followed by actions and accountability specifics in the next section.

Here is a brief example of goals, plans, and resources from a team member named Tim who has been successfully mentored through the *Life/Work Victory* process:

GOALS/PLANS/RESOURCES (GPR)

	Goals	Plans	Resources
Faith	Allocate time to know God	Implement the 3Ds of Daily Excellence Implement weekly Sabbath day	Heaven Heart Hands
Fitness	*Overall Fitness Goal: To be integrated in all three areas.*		
Spirit	Increase real-time communication with God	Abundance of the Moment meditation Study plans Dream Culture	ibethel.org jesusculture.com itbn.org idreamculture.com
Mind	Reprogramming my mind	*How To Hear The Voice of God* *Who Switched Off My Brain?*	cwgministries.org drleaf.com
Body	Increase strength by 20% in six months	Work out 3x per week Maintain hydration, nutrition, and sleep	fitnessanywhere. com beachbody.com superfoodsrx.com
Family	Love/appreciate wife Allocate family time Dream/plan with children	Kiss spouse 3x per day Sunday = Family day Meeting with children	family.org lovingonpurpose. com moralrevolution. com
Future	Earn 20% more in 12 months Invest 5% of work week on professional development Travel to one new country per year	Prepare professional development plan Schedule study time Initiate International opportunities	careerbuilder.com mindtools.com linkedin.com slideshare.net michaelhyatt.com

	Goals	Plans	Resources
Finance	Eliminate 100% of debt in 12 months Increase net-worth by $10K in 16 months Tithe $1K to special project in 12 months	Total Money Makeover Investor's Business Daily Be intentional about money management	daveramsey.com investors.com mint.com prosperoussoul. com
Friends	Allocate three hours for accountability meetings each week Increase e-mail response time to 24 hours Play tennis once a week	Schedule activity and execute	anywhere
Fun	Play more Laugh more Smile more	No metrics	anywhere

Figure 16

In the following pages, you will be introduced to a number of practical and sustainable tools that will help you effect life change.

Please visit www.RestlessTheBook.com for printable versions of these templates.

Now it is your turn...

GOALS/PLANS/RESOURCES (GPR)

	Goals	Plans	Resources
Faith			
Fitness	*Overall Fitness Goal: To be integrated in all three areas.*		
Spirit			
Mind			
Body			
Family			
Future			
Finance			
Friends			
Fun			

Figure 17

Get your dreams dressed and ready. They are about to happen.

Action

Action Item Master (AIM)

A grand canyon exists between a goal and its successful completion. The gap between the goal's starting line and finish line is simply *action*. Sometimes we fall prey to simply talking about doing something, which can cause us to think that we *are* doing it when, in fact, we are not. Always take a reality check and connect with your one thing to overcome yourself and get moving. Action flows from an integrated spirit-mind-body. Action makes molehills out of mountains. Action is the currency of goal attainment. Systemized action will help you to stay focused and sustain your energy.

AIM is a simple tool for action and accountability. Leveraging your completed Goals/Plans/Resources template, you will now prioritize those goals by categorizing them as A, B, or C priorities, for the current season within your *Life Ecosystem*. Each goal is then supported by the AIM, which is activated by listing the prioritized:

Action: What needs to be done to put this goal's plan into action?

Accountable: Who is responsible for carrying out this action?

Attainment: When does this action need to be completed?

Activity: What are the specific action updates?

Life/Work Victory is a step-by-step process. *Abundant Life Victory* requires knowing where you want to be and then mapping the path to get there. Think of this AIM chart as your road map into your *Personal Promised Land*. On the following page you will see a partially filled out chart. This is the AIM for Tim, who filled out the *Goals/Plans/Strategies* chart. His wife, Candess, is his accountability partner:

ACTION ITEM MASTER (AIM)

	Action	Account-ability	Attain-ment	Activity
A-1	30 minutes with God /3Ds of Daily Excellence	Tim	Daily	Ongoing
A-2	Set appt. for Wednesday workout	Tim	Monday	Left voice mail
A-3	Order *RESTLESS*, the new international best seller	Tim	Wednesday	Completed
A-4	Review GPR and budget	Tim/Candess	Saturday	Scheduled
A-5	Paddle boarding date with Candess	Tim	Friday	Booked
B-1	Send in registration form and fee for workshop	Candess	Thursday	Completed
B-2	Lunch with Dennis on Friday	Tim	Wednesday	Scheduled
B-3				
B-4				
B-5				
C-1	Oil Change	Candess	Tuesday	Completed
C-2				
C-3				
C-4				
C-5				

Figure 18

Your turn. Review your GPR. Sync it to your AIM. Your AIM is a process for you and your accountability partner to lead practical and sustainable change.

ACTION ITEM MASTER (AIM)

	Action	Account-ability	Attain-ment	Activity
A-1				
A-2				
A-3				
A-4				
A-5				
B-1				
B-2				
B-3				
B-4				
B-5				
C-1				
C-2				
C-3				
C-4				
C-5				

Figure 19

To activate your goals you will need to check in, both with yourself and your accountability partner, on an ongoing basis. Check in with yourself by spending ten minutes at the start of the day looking over your AIM and ten minutes at the end of the day doing your recap and making adjustments for the next day. Check in with your accountability partner by establishing a weekly meeting. Ask for honest and constructive feedback. Over time and building upon success, you will modify your schedule to meet semi-monthly.

As you implement these *Life/Work Victory* actions, your *Life Ecosystem* will flourish. Remember: *You* run your life business. Only after you have entered and cultivated your *Personal Promised Land* can you successfully enter and cultivate your *Professional Promised Land*. . . .

PART THREE

Professional Promised Land Playbook

Culture:
The Margin of Victory

In Part Two you learned how to enter your *Personal Promised Land*. You are now at the gate of your *Professional Promised Land*. Your *Professional* (or work) *Promised Land* is a plot of land within your *Personal Promised Land*. Your *Professional Promised Land* helps you fulfill and resource your *Abundant Life Victory*. This land's fertility is predicated upon culture. Part Three focuses on creating a revolutionary environment where talents flourish via process and profit. I share fully proven, replicable success models from a multitude of start-up and turnaround projects within all sizes of workplace environments.

A note before I continue: When I speak to "you" in Part Three, I am speaking to both the leaders in a work environment and the team members who work with those leaders. All of you have leadership capacity, even if you are not officially leading your organization, so when I address leaders, I am addressing the work culture as a whole. By "work culture," I refer to any organization where people are working together.

Global business leaders from Apple Inc. to Zappos are attributing their success to culture.[7] Google Inc. employs a chief culture officer and acknowledges the company's unique culture as the foundation of its success. Beyond companies headquartered in America, culture is a force multiplier around the globe. Of course, culture is not limited to the Fortune 500 companies; millions of small-to-medium-sized businesses, like those in the Inc. 500, seek a distinctive culture as their competitive advantage in the workplace.

After years of extensive start-up and turnaround project experience, I have learned that culture is a "root" driver of success; however, many businesses want to go to the next level and focus primarily on competitive strategy — which *is* vital. But what if the work culture is flawed? A flawed culture must be reinvented. The answer to how lies under the soil at the root level of trust, communication, vision, training, planning/process, accountability, and a core focus on people.

I was recently helping a client move into a new building, and our collaboration centered on the lobby display. The natural thing to do was to display the product line, but then it hit us: the product is the people. We found a creative way to honor the company's people instead of its products. Culture is actually the outcome, so let's reverse engineer the process for creating a victorious professional development culture. From my proprietary *Work Culture Victory* solutions, I share the *10 Culture Commandments*, which set new standards:

1. Culture = PEOPLE
People create the culture, so the condition of your people is the condition of your culture. People are much more than commodities

in business; they are the lifeblood. Business is meant to be both fun and a way to solve needs while earning a profit. Yet in some cases, money has moved from medium to master.

Culture is alive. It is constantly moving either toward more life or toward death. I am confident that leaders are innovating new ways to value all people. People are the only infinitely scalable asset in the workplace. People are the greatest competitive advantage in a business if they are properly cultivated. If you must constantly drive your people like cattle, then you will always have to keep them surrounded. If you learn to lead them by drawing them into a vision alignment that blesses their *Abundant Life Victory* as integrated with company goals, they will exceed your expectations. Your *Professional Promised Land* flourishes when it is established upon a cultural foundation of power and love.

2. Cultivate = LOVE PEOPLE

Love for life and people is what drives great cultures. Do you want to truly make the world a better place? Simple: love your people. We are not talking about a weak form of love; we are talking about the strongest form of love that draws out their very greatness from deep within. Your team comes before the customer. Love them first, and they will love the customer. Love involves sacrifice, which is a key ingredient in building a thriving community. Take care of your people, and the tide of your organization will rise and all stakeholder boats with it.

3. Cultivator = LEADER

The ultimate accountability for a culture's success starts and stops with the one person who has the highest degree of accountability for the overall organization. Leaders and culture shapers are at every point in an organization; however, the overall leader sets the tone and holds the entire team accountable for honoring the code of the culture. As an acronym, a LEADER looks like this:

Led — True leaders know who leads them. From whom or where do they source and sustain their power and love? Their *One Thing Motive* will define the character of the culture they are leading.

Empower — A true leader authentically empowers his/her people. He/she knows how to build a team of role players who complement each other. The leader's talent to identify, inspire, train, manage, and retain talent is what empowers people. You cannot empower people without taking a risk on them.

Accountable — The leader understands the top line/bottom line vision, values, goals, measures, and rewards, and communicates them in an ongoing fashion. (A bit further on, you will find proven tools that work within a culture for effective communication.) The team is like a family. If one team member is not doing his/ her job, that member is stealing food off the plate of another team member.

Destiny — The leader lives a workplace life dedicated to the *Abundant Life Victory* of the team. What are the team's dreams and goals? The workplace helps to bring those dreams to life. As team members and leaders achieve individual victory in their lives, they increase corporate victory in the workplace.

Encourage — In all scenarios, the leader leads from a central point of encouragement. It is vital to thank team members for their work, mentor them regarding improvement, and speak life into their futures. The acid test of encouragement is how the leader treats team members when they make costly mistakes. In my teams, I honor well-motivated risks or mistakes that did not work and leverage them as learning platforms. The only fatal transgression is anything that is done to intentionally hurt the team or any individual within the team. Encouragement also means stretching people beyond their comfort zones and pulling them past their perceived limitations into greatness.

Role Model — Imagine that all team members constantly have a video camera focused on the leader at work. The leader's actions will transcend what he or she says. The leader's personal *Abundant Life Victory* model sends messages to the team at a professional level. Only from a place of personal victory can you create professional victory. The leader sets the standard for integrity and enforces an anti-gossip culture. Gossip kills culture, and the grapevine has broadband speed in any organization.

For a rare look at proven, no-nonsense leadership, check out Colin Powell's presentation, "A Leadership Primer." Here is what he says about selecting people to be on your team:

> *Look for intelligence and judgment, and most critically, a capacity to anticipate, to see around corners. Also look for loyalty, integrity, a high energy drive, a balanced ego, and the drive to get things done. How often do our recruitment and hiring processes tap into these attributes? More often than not, we ignore them in favor of length of resume, degrees and prior titles. A string of job descriptions a recruit held yesterday seem to be more important than who one is today, what they can contribute tomorrow, or how well their values mesh with those of the organization. You can train a bright, willing novice in the fundamentals of your business fairly readily, but it's a lot harder to train someone to have integrity, judgment, energy, balance, and the drive to get things done. Good leaders stack the deck in their favor right in the recruitment phase.* [8]

4. "Culturees" = FAMILY

What is the ripple effect of your professional culture? How are marriages and families doing as a result of that culture? The workplace cannot and should not take accountability for a team member's personal life. However, since most people invest more of their lives at work than at home, work leaders are in a powerful position to influence the home culture. Work is about much more than work. Business is about much more than business. Work is about life — the lives of your team members and their families.

5. Culture Ripple Effect = WORLD

Work culture influences home culture. Home culture influences community culture, which influences the city, state, nation, and world. Indeed, the economic engine is a very powerful force for shaping our global quality of life. Remember: culture is driven by the highest-implemented motive of the leader. I am beginning to see innovative breakthroughs; cultures of fear and greed are being replaced by cultures of faith and generosity. A flourishing work culture produces strong self-esteem in its workers, as well as a collective wealth creation and distribution potential to change the world.

6. Culture Cross Training = DIVERSITY

Work is becoming increasingly diverse as a direct result of varied lifestyles and accelerating globalization. Everyone is to be respected and held to the same standard. A consistent culture is paramount for success. No discrimination, harassment, or misuse of work time is tolerated. The corporate vision is the *One Thing/* highest-implemented motive that binds all together. We are all human beings seeking significance in our lives. We all desire to fulfill our infinite potentials and destinies.

7. Culture Metrics = RETURN ON INVESTMENT (ROI)

Culture drives business performance. Culture is much more than traditional vision and values, which we will cover later. The health of a corporation's finances lies in direct proportion to the health of its culture. As oxygen is to the body, profit is to the business. Corporate and individual metrics in healthy work cultures will also expand success beyond the bottom line. Justin Fox writes in the *Harvard Business Review:*

> *Money isn't everything. But for measuring national success, it has long been pretty much the only thing (other than, of course, sports). The specific metric that has prevailed since World War II is the dollar value of a country's economic output, expressed first as gross national product, later as gross domestic product (GDP). . . . Many things of value in life cannot be captured by GDP, but they can be measured by metrics of health, education, and freedom.*[9]

Knowing, and working to achieve, the metrics of your work culture will create (and go beyond) financial success.

8. Culture Capital = INNOVATION

The sheer pace of life and work today, combined with the ambiguity of an ever-changing landscape, creates magnificent opportunities to shape the future. The cultures that can harness the power of the current generation's creativity and marry it with the wisdom and discipline of seasoned workers will win. As Curtis R. Carlson, president and CEO of the Stanford Research Institute observes:

> *In the current economy, 80 percent of all job creation is going on in companies less than five years old. In 1920, the average length of life for a Fortune 500 company was ninety-five years. Today the average life of a Fortune 500 company is twenty years. An*

effective innovation economy requires an innovation ecosystem made up of business, government, capital, and education. The innovative mindset has to permeate throughout the framework of an economy.[10]

Pursue, encourage, foster, and reward innovation.

9. Culture Composting = CHANGE

A thriving culture is one in a constant state of decomposing and recomposing itself, in other words: an ongoing growth cycle of death and rebirth. Just as the healthy human body is in a constant state of cell turnover, the healthy work culture is constantly regenerating itself. This is why empowered, flat, organizational design (an empowered workforce vs. too much hierarchy) is vital for ground-up change. Change is also important for creating an atmosphere that embraces contrarian points of view as long as they support the overarching corporate vision. Too much concern over protocol, saving face, and political correctness can stunt growth and create unhealthy groupthink. Training on constructive collaboration and conflict resolution is vital for sustainable change.

Today, we see multiple "work culture drivers" trending and shaping innovative cultures that are ahead of the curve. These drivers present real-time challenges and opportunities. Culture composting (organic change and regeneration) is the way of life for your victory work culture. Here are samples of work culture drivers:

People as a Priority — Releasing latent human capital productivity.

Millennial Generation Leaders — Thinking differently about life-and-work integration.

Information Generation — Orchestrate collaboration via the cloud and new apps.

Multi-Generation Innovation — Creating wisdom and creative, strategic alliances.

Quality of Life Expectations — Serving the complete *Life Ecosystem.*

Workplace Diversity — Honoring varied global lifestyles.

Global Economy — Leveraging the flat, virtual, and connected world.

These are all leading trends that are shaping work culture. Ask yourself how you want to see these drivers shape *your* work culture and how you will be a part of that shaping.

10. Culture Accountability = CULTURE OF ONE

The ultimate accountability in the workplace rests with the leader. Once leaders have done their jobs, it is up to the team to carry the day. A team member or leader can change the work culture from anywhere within the organization. Once you passionately link to your work culture's vision, you can focus on how you will help make it come true. Sometimes, you may feel like you do not matter, but the truth is that you can greatly affect the atmosphere around you. Your attitude and *Life/Work Victory* power will give you the long-term energy to encourage your peers. Look for ways to improve work processes and then communicate those processes. The top work cultures in the world understand and encourage the culture of one.

The

V*s*

of Victory

Voice

Vision

Values

Value-Added

Validators

Vortex

Velocity

Work As an Adventure

Work as an adventure fulfills us, prospers us, and adds value to the world around us. Work as an adventure prioritizes faith and generosity over fear and greed. Work as an adventure optimizes team delight, customer delight, and shareowner delight.

Do you have a work dream you'd like to pursue? Do you want to take your current business to greater heights? The process of a culture's start-up or turnaround is a combination of art and science. Such processes can be daunting. I've tried them from every angle and finally developed tools for creating a victory work culture. This highly practical and sustainable third set of *Optimizers* focus on profitable team building as well as talent management.

VOICE

In the LEADER section we saw that a leader is led by a *One Thing Motive:* the source of the voice that draws them in and drives them. As a leader of your own life and work, it is important to know who is leading you and how to be an active listener. How you are led is how you lead.

You will notice that this process interfaces with the *Personal Promised Land* section of Part Two. Personal purpose and priorities will define professional purpose and priorities. A leader's source will define the leader, which will define the culture.

As a leader you must first flourish in your internal environment. The leader works from inside-out and the culture responds from the outside-in. Individual voice is customized for corporate success.

The voice I listen to for inspiration, insight, and instruction is:

....

....

....

VISION

My gift is to see and release the hidden, infinite potential in individuals and corporations. When I am engaged in a start-up or turnaround project, I focus on a vision statement that is twofold. First of all, it addresses the work culture. Secondly, it addresses the specific marketplace performance. For example, an organization might define its prioritized purpose in a vision statement like: *To create an environment where talents flourish while exceeding corporate growth goals.*

Sometimes, people confuse vision and mission. Vision is where you want to go and mission is what you want to do. I focus on vision first and then define mission in the business plan. The business plan will define the strategy and tactics to make it happen.

Vision Line of Sight/zero conflicts between the CEO and frontlines is ensured via the Goals/Measures/Rewards (GMR) process. The GMR communication/accountability process is one of the single greatest tools to lead and manage work culture excellence. GMR templates are also shared on our website.

My work culture's twofold vision statement is:

VALUES

Values complement the vision and are living words. They must be role-modeled on a daily basis, and the entire team is accountable to them. The recent U.S. sub-prime mortgage meltdown and corresponding global economic effects were due in great part to a crisis in values. Misguided values led to the misuse of financial products. The economic hit was the outcome of a poor value system. Such a scenario is an example of what can happen when leaders skew their values and serve themselves before others. Values align with vision and the highest purpose of the work.

Leaders have the responsibility to live and model a healthy and clearly communicated set of values.

Bill Hybels, innovative business and church leader and CEO of Willow Creek Community Church, explains the need to articulate values:

> *The very best leaders I know wrestle with words until they are able to communicate their big ideas in a way that captures the imagination, catalyzes actions, and lifts spirits. They coin creeds and fashion slogans and create rallying cries, all because they understand that language matters.*[11]

> *Great leaders know that when they assemble teams around them, they can't merely assign tasks for people to check off a list. Instead, they must launch an all-out DNA-infusion campaign to make sure everyone is on the same "values" page.*[12]

For years I have led with this simple yet profound set of governing core values for a successful workplace — TEAM:

Trust — Everything is built on this, which translates to honesty and respect among all team members.

Encouragement — Everything is done from a place of encouragement and forward motion.

Accountability — Everyone is accountable for meritocracy-based, measurable results.

Mentoring — Everyone receives ongoing mentoring to optimize one's present and future professional growth.

I would like to add a bit more about mentoring. The *Harvard Business Review* recently published an article entitled, "Why Top Young Managers Are in a Nonstop Job Hunt." Listen to what surveys revealed:

Workers reported that companies generally satisfy their needs for on-the-job development and that they value these opportunities, which include high-visibility positions and significant increases in responsibility. But they're not getting much in the way of formal development, such as training, mentoring, and coaching — things they also value highly.[13]

Great leaders create great teams. Together, they create great businesses. Here are a few of my favorite professional values by leaders of highly successful businesses:

The Cook doctrine by Tim Cook, Apple CEO, regarding his vision/values and the Steve Jobs legacy:

We believe that we are on the face of the earth to make great products, and that's not changing. We are constantly focusing on innovating. We believe in the simple not the complex. We believe that we need to own and control the primary technologies behind the products that we make, and participate only in markets where we can make a significant contribution. We believe in saying no to thousands of projects, so that we can really focus on the few that are truly important and meaningful to us. We believe in deep collaboration and cross-pollination of our groups, which allow us to innovate in a way that others cannot. And frankly, we do not settle for anything less than excellence in every group in the company, and we have the self-honesty to admit when we're wrong and the courage to change. And I think, regardless of who is in what job, those values are so embedded in this company that Apple will do extremely well.[14]

Inside Apple's Culture: 10 Ways to Think Different[15]

1. Empower employees to make a difference.
2. Value what's important, not minutiae.
3. Love and cherish the innovators.
4. Do everything important internally.
5. Get marketing.
6. Control the message.
7. Little things make a big difference.
8. Do not make people do things, make them better at doing things.
9. When you find something that works, keep doing it.
10. Think different.

Google: Ten Things We Know to be True[16]

1. Focus on the user and all else will follow.
2. It's best to do one thing really, really well.
3. Fast is better than slow [in regard to search results].
4. Democracy on the web works.
5. You do not need to be at your desk to need an answer.
6. You can make money without doing evil.
7. There's always more information out there.
8. The need for information crosses all borders.
9. You can be serious without a suit.
10. Great just isn't good enough.

What are the values of your work culture?

....

....

....

....

....

....

VALUE-ADDED

The traditional idea of "value-added" is that the value of your product or service will be greater than its cost. In a work culture, this definition includes variables that transcend the cultural status quo and deliver a competitive advantage. These advantages can be nonlinear and intangible, yet they are vital to the success of the business. Value-added represents the X factor, or that which provides the extra edge that makes people and teams great. Here are a few examples of communities who understand and operate from a value-added work culture:

Immigrant Community — This is one of my favorites because in one way or another, we are all immigrants. This value-added trait is one that never settles for comfort zones and always seeks a better country and experience. This community lights a fire that burns within cultures to truly change the world. It is willing to pay the price for greatness. We can all trace our roots to those who came before us, those who paid a dear price for our freedoms and opportunities. Sometimes, the generations that enjoy the fruits of their forefathers' risk and labor can fall into an entitlement mode.

I am not suggesting that we needlessly toil, but we do need to remember who helped get us where we are and then build upon their achievements. My very own grandmother emigrated from Italy to America at the age of sixteen. Alone and unable to speak the English language, she sailed past the Statue of Liberty and arrived at Ellis Island in New York to fight for a new and better life. I reap the benefit of her legacy while continuing to grow it for my own children's children. A healthy immigrant mentality is a powerful driving force in building a value-added culture.

Miracle Community — A few years ago, some of our team members created a prayer club in the office of a highly accountable, performance-based start-up business. The goal of the prayer club was to honor God with the first fruits of each week by meeting at 7:00 AM every Monday morning. The club was entirely voluntary, and not all team members chose to participate. The club was diligent in following the laws of that particular state and did not harass, discriminate, or utilize company time. The results of that prayer time were otherworldly. The work culture was drawn forward by a rare love and respect for one another, as well as increased grace and excellence. Team members would go for prayer walks during breaks and pray for knowledge and wisdom regarding their work. On their desks, they kept Bibles opened to favorite Scripture verses. This prayer club's members found their God to be a God of great business ingenuity and acumen. By holding business meetings with their God, they were able to practically apply new power and revelation into daily operations. Miracles of creativity and business results streamed through this environment. The atmosphere changed lives, families, and an entire community. Industry benchmarks proved that they were 30-90 percent more productive in key performance indicators.

A Spirit-led business can be reflected in the numbers. In the natural, those astounding numbers did not make sense to the experts in this field. However, God and business worked in perfect harmony through that particular value-added culture. That miracle community was composed of Christian team members, yet visitors from a diversity of faiths have toured it to learn new practices for maximizing productivity.

Collaboration Community — Apple Inc. has a single profit and loss process for the company, which drives its high collaboration community. Google Inc. and the 3M Company give team members between 15-20 percent of their weekly work time to focus on their creative passions for the business. Google also has company-wide "TGIF" meetings each Friday, where all workers openly collaborate with their leaders. Pixar uses a system named "plussing," which empowers team members to offer constructive insight during feedback sessions while also always finding encouraging "plus-embedded" comments. With turnaround projects, I have consistently found individual and team productivity levels to be sub-optimized at the 60-70 percent of potential range. Through culture renewal, business planning/process improvements radically increase individual and team productivity. Imagine that all workers in your workplace were simply 10 percent more productive; imagine the collective productivity that would burst forth in your organization's value to all stakeholders. Productivity increases are linked to culture optimization. Culture optimization is linked to renewed beliefs. Renewed beliefs lead to new behaviors and actions. New actions will equal new results. I once had an opportunity to lead a team that grew a customer membership community by approximately thirty times its size in three years. That team revolutionized an industry, and their achievement was attained by fully leveraging unity and shared resources. The root source of productivity increase is renewed beliefs leading to new behaviors leading to new results. Valued-added culture is a foundational, competitive advantage in business.

VALIDATORS

"If you can't measure it, you can't manage it."
— Peter Drucker, Management Innovator.

Culture is about more than posting a vision, mission, and values on a banner. Culture is the lifeblood of an environment and is measured by a rich variety of metrics. Each culture's scenario is unique, but there are some standard best practices, culture processes, and tools that work across cultures to help you succeed professionally. Though these processes and tools are customized for each project, I've included a sample list of cultural best practices in the form of processes and tools.

Let's begin with a proven sub-set of *Optimizers* that are vital to your victory work culture:

The 7Cs of Champions
(Selection and Development Optimizers)

"Champion selection," or the hiring of team members, might appear to be a leader-specific topic. However, even if you are the newest hire working the graveyard shift, you need to know what a successful leader is looking for, and you need to know how to be that person. Here are seven workplace optimizers a leader should take into account before inviting a new player to the team:

CULTURE

Again, culture = people. Hire and groom champions and you will have a champion culture. Next to establishing the work culture, the selection and development of champions is the leader's most important job.

A champion culture is a force multiplier, which means that the atmosphere raises everyone up to increasing standards of excellence. New team members must fit the chemistry of the team's culture. An "A" player is 10 to 100 times more valuable to an organization than a mediocre team member. I am defining an "A" player as a person with the team attitude, disciplined work ethic, specific talents, and the right culture fit. Choosing champion team members may or may not have anything to do with their experience or other traditional hiring factors.

Great work cultures produce great leaders. Successful team members align their visions and values with those of the CEO and know that they are empowered and rewarded for continual productivity and innovation. Work is a sacred covenant between the CEO and those people on the frontlines. Great leaders understand what is most important to everyone on the team, individually and collectively. A leader sets the vision and values and allocates resources, while also protecting and promoting the team members. Great work cultures do not drive people like cattle; great work cultures draw people forward into greatness. Because many workplaces operate with a selfish culture instead of a selfless one, they are sub-optimized. When you heal an unhealthy culture, you create a healthy environment where you optimize your business breakthroughs.

What can you do right now to improve the culture at your workplace?

....

....

....

....

....

....

....

....

....

....

....

CHARACTER

Champions are truthful. Character can be distilled into a single word: truth. Truth = trust and integrity. Trust is mandatory to build and lead a successful team. Are you a truthful person? Can you be trusted? Will you admit to mistakes? Will you place team victory ahead of personal glory? Will you openly assist teammates? Will you connect your passionate desires to the vision and values of your workplace to see victory at home and work? The answers to all of these questions share something in common: the discipline to behave as you believe, to do as you say. Great cultures are highly disciplined cultures, and character is the result of discipline. Choose people of discipline to join your team. Discipline training is also a vital part of work culture success. Discipline can be taught when the right incentives are in place.

In Part Two, you clarified your purpose, priorities, time, goals, and actions. Successfully establishing those in your personal life helps you to succeed in your professional life. You achieve extreme success at work when you pay disciplined attention to detail. Furthermore, when you achieve success in one area of work, it can be replicated in other areas. My project management teams create success books — digital binders that document every imaginable detail that contributed to the win; these books lay the railroad tracks to success. When you invite a new worker to contribute to that success, you are adding the art of his/her personality to the science of process, thereby mitigating the risks and optimizing the rewards. You can further reduce risk by hiring new workers who demonstrate solid character.

Character is absolutely mandatory to steward talent. Character can be unlearned and relearned and is forged over time. The highest level of character is consistent with the highest-performing cultures. If you lead a work culture, you are responsible for living and demonstrating that highest level of character. Character begets productivity, and we are known by our fruit not by our gifts.

We lead by example. Whatever your leadership role, do a character check. What needs fixing? How can you grow into the person you want to become?

....

....

....

....

....

....

....

....

....

....

....

COMPETENCE

Champions get the job done and done well. How do you find the best team members? Every hiring choice will present risks. A team member's core competencies might be easy to identify for one position and more challenging for another. Competence requirements vary according to the job. To validate competence, use a disciplined process of multiple meetings, off-resume/CV references, and situational interviews. To help lessen risk, use referrals whenever possible. Some positions provide an opportunity for competence to grow through on-the-job training. Keep in mind that an initial combination of talent and character can open the door to greater competence.

Work culture victory requires you to train team members in how to take dominion over their jobs. Dominion thinking is knowing that you can and will dominate the playing field as a member of your team and culture. Like members of a sports team, they practice over and over until every play becomes second nature.

During training, team members need to experience their culture's real-life scenarios with the support and encouragement of an assigned mentor. Such a supervised development period of wins and losses will accelerate the learning curve for every new member of the team. Once integrated into the team, each member then benefits from ongoing training, which builds confidence that is vital for victory. Leaders need to model this continual learning process by consistently adding to their own "game."

How can you adopt an ongoing, self-paced program of professional development?

COMMUNICATION

Champions are efficient and effective communicators. By communication, I am referring not only to speaking skills but also to the art of listening. You listen to what your spirit is telling you, to what business is happening on top of the table, and to what is happening under the table (e.g. savvy awareness of power positioning.) Active listening is an absolutely vital success factor. People tend to see things through the lenses of their own perceptions. I cannot tell you how many times I have summarized notes and action items at the conclusion of a conference call only to find gaps that had to be filled because someone had not listened. In addition to listening, the ability to speak in an honest, open, and direct manner is critical. Communicating well is the combination of excellent word choice, tonality, and body language. People who can articulate what they will do for the team, and what they want will win. Effective listening and speaking styles will directly translate to the written word.

Communication excellence is essential for the inevitable conflict resolution demands that will arise in any thriving culture. Conflict resolution must be a communication process priority used to empower people to productively face small and large issues. Leaders can maintain a culture's communication by practicing "management by walking around" (MBWA) to take the pulse of the team. Finally, a deliberate and cost-effective training process is an integral part of grooming champions for sustainable communication excellence.

How can you improve your culture-enriching communication skills?

....

....

....

....

....

....

....

....

....

....

....

CRITICAL THINKING

Champions are thinkers. Champions wisely evaluate the constant barrage of real-time data, information, and knowledge. As a society, we have moved from an agrarian to industrial to information age. We now face the challenge and opportunity of what to do with all this information. What information is and is not relevant to our lives and work? How do we manage it? How do we control it, so it does not control us? We are poised on the threshold of a new era of true wisdom-seeking, which will require critical thinking and a Socratic (question-led) style. Critical thinking is the intentional focus of thoughts through a particular idea, concept, or option. The process involves listening to your intuition and using your mind. If you are a praying person, then pray about situations as you think them through. I also focus on discernment as a specific skill in our team-building projects. Identifying purpose, priorities, and time helps us to make optimum decisions.

Remember that you are seeking an *Abundant Life Victory*. When I speak with potential team members, I help them think through their new job opportunities. We analyze how the complete overall package of a position transcends compensation and title. We look at the job through the panoramic lens of their *7Fs of Freedom*. I help them think through these as they consider their new work culture, family adjustments, quality of life variables, and commute/travel factors. How will the new position support their life purposes? What are their real needs, wants, and priorities?

When you think critically, you consider all the options. Too many times, a highly talented worker becomes reactive instead of proactive. Excellent critical thinking leads to optimized discernment and decision-making. Some people struggle with both. It is important to remember the Purpose/Priorities/Time/Goals/Actions process and the *7Fs of Freedom* to make the right life and work decisions that attract success. I have found that profits increase when team members are professionally trained to develop a productive grid for making excellent decisions. To enter and grow in your *Personal* and *Professional Promised Land*, you will be blessed by scheduling time to stop and think about the why, what, and how of your life and work.

Challenge yourself to dedicate a segment of time each week to critical thinking. When will you schedule a consistent time to turn off the all-digital, all-the-time lifestyle and give yourself the blessed gift of quiet time to reflect?

....

....

....

COMPETITIVE EDGE

Champions are edgy in their own unique and productive way. All of the champions I have worked with have had a competitive edge — that one talent trait that sets them apart from the crowd. A competitive edge empowers people to rise above circumstances and compete at a higher level. Many times this talent trait simply comes in the form of perseverance. Perseverance for excellence manifests as an unshakable belief system backed by intense and sustained action, which delivers extraordinary results. These champions are the special ones. Even when they do not feel like it, they wake up and work. What a marvelous thing it is to not just overcome the self but to rise above it. People who do this desire to fully and forever honor the precious gift of life. They transcend their work. The competitive edge is directly connected to the *One Thing Motive* introduced in Part Two. We have to know our personal purpose to have professional success.

Great leaders intuitively know how to build a team whose whole is greater than its parts. If you want a truly great team, you will have to take risks when hiring people and building teams. Game breakers have that intangible, contrarian X factor that may not fit the norm. I call it the "personal extreme" factor (in a good way) because everyone has it in one way or another. Rather than suppress it, I like to celebrate it and leverage the "personal extreme" factor for the good of the team.

Great cultures, teams, and individuals also know how to adapt and bounce back after facing challenges. They know how to turn mountains into molehills and cement barriers into speed bumps. I love the *hutzpah* (boldness) and *davka* (despite everything) traits of the Israeli culture. Despite what happens to the Israelis, they respond with an uncanny boldness that leads to even greater prosperity. Perseverance under pressure yields mature leaders, teams, and cultures.

What is your competitive edge? How can you rekindle that fire that burns inside of you to create a better life?

CAREER DEVELOPMENT

Champions have a burning desire to get ahead in life. They flourish in an environment that has a defined career development plan. Career development is an often under-managed component of building a sustainable victory work culture. Workers need something to look forward to. Career development can be in the form of a defined career path; it can also come in the form of a simple **Job Refresher Plan** such as:

Ongoing Training — Industry workshops or work-related book clubs.

Cross Training — Simple time allocation to learn about other interconnected jobs.

Atmosphere Diversification — Out-of-office activities such as visiting customers, attending trade shows, even going for a walk.

Special Project Assignments — Special task teams rewarded for their work by being empowered to drive frontline innovation.

Approved Workplace Clubs — Lunchtime gatherings to explore similar interests and/or professional development.

Approved De-Stressors — Anything from stretching breaks, health food in the office kitchen, Nerf guns, office plants, art on the walls, etc.

Approved Thank-You Rewards — Creative, non-monetary rewards: the gift of work time to volunteer in the community, personal mental health days, special situational bonuses to take a spouse/date out to dinner.

To generate the best career development ideas for your work

culture, you might consider appointing a culture champion to serve as a bridge between the CEO and the frontlines. By investing attention and time in keeping workers happy, you will reap long-term profit growth. Creating an environment that flourishes is in direct opposition to the law of diminishing returns (working more and getting less done). Simple cultural strategies like the *Job Refresher Plan* can powerfully boost productivity and quality of life.

What ideas do you have to develop your personal career and your workplace in general?

Here is a sample of the *Work Culture Victory* toolkit available online at our website:

Mirror — You are accountable for your actions.

Position Description/Compensation Plan — Cornerstone tool (job overview, responsibilities, interfaces, qualifications, and pay for performance).

On-Boarding/Retention Program — Customized initial and ongoing training.

Professional Development Plan (PDP) — Cornerstone tool (professional/personal training/career goals, plans, resources).

Goals/Measures/Rewards (GMR) — Cornerstone tool (work report card integrated with the PDP).

Annual Business Plan/Ultimate User Experience Cycle (UUX) — Business strategy/road map.

Quarterly Business Plans (QBP) — Provides focus and accountability.

Weekly Reports/Meetings — Efficient tracking and communication.

Executive Dashboards — Real-time information (analytics) on vital customer, financial, sales, and project metrics.

Culture Index — "People metrics" for team member delight on morale, productivity, turnover, ideas, and growth.

Following are examples of what some of the tools for the PDP and GMR look like:

PROFESSIONAL DEVELOPMENT PLAN (PDP)

Team Member:	*Last*	*First*	*Initials*	Manager	
Position Title:				Assess-ment Period:	

Performance Summary

Summarize accomplishments vs. goals in the past one year review period. Specify net accountability and achievement via quantifiable metrics.

Vision/Values Summary
Summarize how you accomplish your goals
Evaluate your performance in terms of the Team Vision and Values:

Create an Environment where Talents Flourish
Trust, Encouragement, Accountability, Mentoring

Career Development Summary

Strengths: Describe your strengths. How have you improved over the past year?	
Development: Identify the most critical performance/values development needs and specific action plans to address.	
Professional Goals: List job enhancement opportunities. If you desire a job change, list preferences including job title, department/function, and timing. *Personal Goals:* (Optional)	

Signed		**Date**

Team Member

Signed		**Date**

Team Member

Figure 20

GOALS/MEASURES/REWARDS (GMR)

Name:		Date:	
Title:		Dept:	

Goals (How do/will you contribute to these goals?)	Weight	Rating	Weight-ed Score

1. Work Culture
 	
• Create an Environment Where Talents Flourish
 	
• Demonstrate the **TEAM** commit-ment of:
 	
   o **T**rust
   o **E**ncouragement
   o **A**ccountability
   o **M**entoring
	30%		

2. Financial Growth (Revenue and Profit-ability)	30%		
3. "Customer Delight" • Meet/Exceed Customer Expecta-tions	30%		

4. Team Member Open Objective	10%		

Notes:

Signed		**Date**

Team Member

Signed		**Date**

Team Member

Figure 21

VORTEX

A vortex is the center of a rapidly swirling flow of fluid. What does a vortex have to do with your *Professional Promised Land* and a *Work Culture Victory?* The flow of life and work will include pressure-packed, vortex experiences. The vortex will test the purpose and priorities of a person; it also will test the vision and values of a team and its entire work organization. The combinations of purpose/priorities and vision/values must be strong and solid. Every work culture will face pressure, but the cultures with clearly defined purpose, priorities, vision, and values will withstand it. Interestingly, pressure is minimized at the center of the vortex. The life/work culture that remains calm amid all pressures will endure for victory.

From a vortex's center of power and peace, there are times we must rise up and fight. We live in a constantly changing and competitive world. Work culture change, business start-ups, and turnaround projects have a high degree of unpredictable, nonlinear dynamics. We can make change and competition work for us or let it work against us. A key success factor is planning for the unexpected. Great leaders can see around the corners and ensure that the team is prepared for any situation. A victory culture informs its workers of the most challenging parts of the job up front and prepares its workers to conquer them. The best cultures communicate the challenges and counter-strategies in advance, thereby ensuring preparation.

You can build a margin into your life and work that anticipates change. This strategy is the far-better alternative to redlining (going at maximum speed) all the time with life and work. Maintaining a reserve of spiritual energy, health, family, culture, and financial capital is vital for turning challenges into opportunities. When you are able to do that, you are in position to move in the opposite direction of the herd and to make challenges work in your favor.

Making challenges work for you is somewhat similar to a judo principle in which a fighter takes the opposing force and transfers its energy back onto itself. We can use this strategy in our own thought life to activate 360-degree thinking, which changes thoughts of lack into thoughts of gratitude and expectation. Our lives and work are like interconnected muscle tissue: great tension and stretching results in greater strength and flexibility. By transforming challenges into opportunities, you will, over time, build extraordinary mental toughness.

What powers your calm center? What are your work-related challenges? How can you leverage them and transform them into opportunities for growth and advantage?

VELOCITY

Velocity is the speed and direction of an object in motion. In this definition, you are the object in motion, and the speed and direction refer to your personal and professional life. Your *Professional Promised Land* is always integrated with your *Personal Promised Land*. Your ultimate success in the *7Vs of Victory* is in direct proportion to your empowerment from the *7Fs of Freedom*. You must optimize your Faith/Fitness/Family/Future/Finances/Friends/Fun since they lead your work Voice/Vision/Values/Value-Added/Validators/Vortex/Velocity. We discussed the *Life Ecosystem* in Part Two, which applies here as well. Our life/work trajectory and pace requires a certain tempo for its maximum optimization. If we unnaturally rush or delay the maturation process, we will suffer.

I like to go on hikes and get away from the world by immersing myself in nature. I talk to nature and nature talks back. When I listen with my heart, I hear a symphony of activity: streaming sunlight, flowing water, singing birds, gentle breezes, and moving creatures of all types. Beautiful rhythms and harmonies emerge from this dance of life. There is no rush, no stress, and no anxiety. Perfect peace, order, and productivity live here. This is my model for velocity. All of nature's components know their purpose/priorities and vision/values. Unlike us, they do not have a choice. How can we do more by doing less? How can we work from rest?

The *Life/Work Victory* and *Work Culture Victory* processes are designed to mirror nature's abundant flow of life and work. Like an ecosystem in nature, your *Life Ecosystem* is designed to maximize life to its fullest. However, there is a price to pay for the greatness that results from a fully lived life. You have to receive change, personalize change, and enact change.

A long-term vision + well-managed velocity + a step-by-step plan + built-in margin of grace = success.

Your velocity is a vital part of this process. Most people attempt to do too much on a relatively short timeline and completely underestimate their potential over a longer timeline. Anything is possible . . . over time. Life *is* a race, but it is a marathon instead of a sprint. The outcome is worth it. The outcome is your life exceeding your wildest imagination!

Based upon this book's teaching, how will you adjust your life/work velocity for the utmost life/work victory?

....

....

....

....

....

....

....

....

....

This process works. If you want to see how, read our customer testimonials. They can be found on our website at www. RestlessTheBook.com. Be encouraged, be inspired, be victorious!

Omega

Well Done! You have successfully completed the main body of the book. Thank you for going the distance. Although entitled Omega (ending), this section is actually an Alpha (beginning). At any starting point, it is vital for you to set expectations:

1. You *can* start over. No matter what has occurred in your life up to this point, no matter if you are making minor or major life changes, no matter how you feel, you can start over. When do you begin? Today. Now. This moment. You already said the first "yes" by reading this book. Say the second "yes" by taking the activation steps in the upcoming *Restless* Challenge.

2. You will face trials. I thank God for the material in this book because it helps me to renew my mind every day and to stay renewed through the "everydayness" of life. We are all works in process in a constant state of learning and growth. Sometimes, change breaks through in the miracle of the moment; other times, change breaks through in the miracle of the long hour. The first reality check is that real and sustainable change requires *100%* commitment for *Life/Work Victory* and *Work*

Culture Victory. The second reality check can be found in how we respond when the pressure is on, when things do not go the way that we think they should, or when the change process takes longer than expected. Productive pain is a partner on the path to promotion.

3. You *will* win. If you align your vision with whom you were truly created to be, if you initiate change, embrace pain, and persevere, you will win. Always envision your outcome and keep your eyes on the prize. In fact, the victory is already yours. In each and every part of life and work, the victory is yours! You are simply on a path to take accountability for your destiny and prepare to manage it. This book positions you to create miraculous external results. Even more importantly, it transcends those results for the unfathomable miracle of internal and eternal victory.

Step One: The *Restless* Challenge

For *Life/Work Victory* schedule a summit meeting with your accountability partner/partners to launch your change management process:

- *Purpose (7Rs of Rest)*
- *Priorities (7Fs of Freedom)*
- *Time (GREAT168)*
- *Goals/Action (GPR, AIM)*
- *Customized Solutions*

For *Work Culture Victory* schedule a summit meeting with your accountability partner/partners to launch your change management process:

- *10 Culture Commandments*
- *7Vs of Victory Audit*
- *PDP, GMR Priorities*
- *Work Culture Victory Toolkit*
- *Customized Solutions*

The change process is a long-term lifestyle and work-style commitment. The key is to restart your heart and mind, to have a high character/competence accountability partner and to focus on personalizing a best-practices model for your life/work. Sometimes, I go into the office on a weekend and pretend that the upcoming Monday is the first day of my life or the first day on the job. In that light, how do I see things? What would I change? I pray it and play it forward to create an action-oriented plan.

Step Two: Restless Resources

Stay connected to our research and solutions through our website, RestlessTheBook.com. We are expanding our private practice to work with select individuals and companies. We are specialized individual/corporate talent mentors, training innovators, and turnaround project leaders with a fierce focus on breakthrough results. We believe that the prophetic without the pragmatic is pointless, that an idea without implementation is idle, and that these exercises without execution in real life are empty.

Here is a menu of our workshops and project management:

Life/Work Victory

This workshop/mentoring service focuses on individual and corporate clients. This solution includes an extensive pre-workshop discovery process, a two-day workshop, and follow-though services. We customize the *7Fs of Freedom* to exceed your expectations. On our website, we will also be conducting individual/community mentoring. This *One-on-One Victory* will provide further, customized solutions for our clients.

Work Culture Victory

Also a workshop/mentoring service, *Work Culture Victory* focuses on workplace environments. This solution includes an extensive qualification and discovery phase, a two-day workshop, and quality assurance/mentoring services. Here, too, we customize the *7Vs of Victory* to exceed your expectations. This solution may also take the form of a longer-term, project-management engagement.

Business Development Victory

This customized, project-management service focuses on accelerating the growth ramp for start-up or turnaround businesses. We use a proprietary solution set of culture foundation, financial models and market intelligence/database marketing to create demand and sustainable growth for your business. This solution requires extensive qualification, discovery, and management commitment to ensure long - term success. Our website showcases a few sample tools for *Business Development Victory*.

God and Business Victory

The *God and Business Victory* customized workshop/mentoring solution focuses on *profitably* integrating God and business. We focus on a Father-Business reality check (3A-3Z Biblical Business), avad, Presence/principles, performance/personal best, plan/present, prayer club, anointing/team/model business planning, tri-laboration streaming, St. Peter Principle, and nROE (the gold standard).

God is at the center of all of our work, yet our clients decide whether they want that fact to be public or private when we are working with them. We have built the utmost respect into the product positioning and delivery of our services.

PRODUCT POSITIONING

SOLUTIONS	PUBLIC DELIVERY	PRIVATE DELIVERY	
Personal/Professional Development	Life/Work Victory	Life/Work Victory	Customized Tool Kits for all
Cultural/Business Development	Work Culture Victory Business Development Victory	Work Culture Victory Business Development Victory God and Business	

Figure 22

Acknowledgements

I would like to thank and acknowledge the key players on this team. *Restless* is my first book, and it is very much a family-and-friends project. We all worked together to make it happen.

First and foremost, thank you Father for Jesus my Christ, for Your Holy Spirit, Your Holy Bible, and for Your inspired words in this project as well as for everything in my life. More importantly, thank You for the simple joy of knowing You. I love You beyond my capacity to love You.

Thank you to my bride, Linda, I love you forever and thank you for being my best friend. You are my true joy and trusted advisor in all things. Your grace and beauty is all over this project. Thank you to my most blessed children, Marie and Dominic: your hearts of abundant life are my inspiration each and every day. I also honor Dino, Matilda, Patty and Johnny Sbrocca as well as my cousin, Bill Conlin.

Thank you Anna Elkins, our extraordinary friend, artist, and content editor. You are the embodiment of the book. Your lighthearted elegance and excellence lives in this project and beyond.

We extend our deepest gratitude to our entire book/internet "A" team: Holy Spirit, Linda Sbrocca, Marie Sbrocca, Dominic Sbrocca, Anna Elkins, Andy Hedman, Brad Webster, Lorraine Box, Diana Vader, Stephen Carnes, Daniel Vogler, and Lightning Source.

Thank you to our friends, coworkers, and test pilots: Chad & Christina McCulley, The Marinello Family, Brian Schmitt, Brien Walters, Andy Mason, Scott Putnam, Breanne Watson, Angelo Jeanpierre, Bjorn Greipsland, Edison Chung, Antje Jordan, Aaron Teo Seng Wee, Tim Altero, Mike O'Brien, Rob Moyer, James Kernan, Ana Cho, Erica Gismegian, Akshay Lazarus, Samuel Gichuhi, Philip LaTrobe, Nathan Noble, Sally Bethea Holt, Dennis Mihalka, Kathy Lewis, Sue Mack, Bernice Phillips, Jane Cage, Teresa Annibale, Steve Halland, Cynthia Lacunza, Vanessa Chandler, Sally Hanan, Kelsey Kehoe, Tim Jenne, Aaron McMahon and Maggie Forsythe for your true friendship and encouragement on this project and beyond. Thank you also to all our friends and coworkers who provided testimonials.

Finally, I give it up for all of the students, workers, and leaders at Bethel Church in Redding, California. You are an innovative embassy of Heaven's resources on earth. Thank you to *all* of the spiritual and business leaders who encourage my growth in spirit, soul, and body.

Blessing

Preface

As we come to our close, I cannot help but think about the end of the authorized Steve Jobs' biography. Steve Jobs revolutionized multiple industries/lifestyles and was seeking the ultimate truth until the very end of his life here on this earth. He said:

> *I like to think that something survives after you die. It's strange to think that you accumulate all this experience, and maybe a little wisdom, and it just goes away. So I really want to believe that something survives, that maybe your consciousness endures. But on the other hand, perhaps it's like an on-off switch. Click! And you are gone.*[17]

Is life really like and on-off switch, or is it like an *on-on switch*? Only you can discover this answer for yourself. I encourage you to test my words with an open heart and actually communicate with my God by seeking a personal encounter for your answer.

179

Prayer

Heavenly Father, thank You that Your invitation to enter into Your precious and magnificent promises remains open to all of us. You know all things, so You know exactly what we need; use Your power on our behalf. You are always present; please sync with our hearts now that we may experience You. Change our lives for Your best.

Thank You for Your tender mercy and the new life that is available in fresh supply each day. Your promises help us to conquer the past once and for all. Our past does not equal our future. Healing starts now as we kill any generational curses and all forms of darkness. We destroy wrongful beliefs/associations and replace them with hope and help. Please impart divine courage for taking the first step in the right direction. Thank You for helping us to build momentum into the new day.

Thank You for Your intimacy. Help us reveal ourselves to You that we may know You more. Thank you for helping us to recognize and overcome our own, over-analytical voices and the fear-filled voice of the enemy. Your voice is filled with love, power and spontaneity. Please help us to stop outsourcing our intimacy with You to others. Our oneness with Your voice is the starting point of all things. In You all things build relationship and produce anointed growth in Your time. Truth reigns in our hearts, and You are the key to unlocking the highest expression of freedom.

Thank You for imparting Your blueprint for *Abundant Life Victory* to all who will receive it. We agree to open the gift and test it. As stated in the Alpha, it is time to *raise the living* to a new standard! We can have *Life/Work Victory* in a personalized way that introduces us to a taste of heavenly peace here and now.

Thank You for Your *Abundance of the Moment*. No matter what happens, we experience unexplainable beauty in knowing and loving You forever. Right here and right now, knowing You is everything. Knowing that your crown of thorns created a crown of new life for us. Experiencing this knowledge is restful productivity, and we are fully empowered to live it out.

Thank You for releasing Your power in this blessing through the living Messiah, Jesus Christ. And finally, thank You for fulfilling Your promises as we seek, find, and live Your *Rest.*

ABUNDANCE OF THE MOMENT

Figure 23

Endnotes

1   Henry David Thoreau, Walden, (New York: Fall River Press, 2008), 6.

2   Anne Frank, *Anne Frank: Diary of a Young Girl: The Definitive Edition.* (New York: Bantam, 1997), iPad edition.

3   Augustine, *The Confessions of St. Augustine,* (Grand Rapids: Spire, 2008), 19.

4   Bill Johnson quote, "This Is Grace" Podcast, July 15, 2012.

5   Robin Furneaux, *William Wilberforce* (London: Hamish Hamilton, 1974), 37.

6   Caroline Leaf, *Who Switched off my Brain?* (Nashville: Thomas Nelson, 2009), 19.

7   The beliefs, customs, practices, and social behavior of a particular nation or people.

8   Colin Powell, SlideShare, "A Leadership Primer." http://www.slideshare.net/guesta3e206/colin-powells-leadership-presentation.

9   Justin Fox, "The Economics of Well-Being." *Harvard Business Review.* January-February. (2012): 80 and 83.

10   Dr. Curtis R. Carlson, "Innovation" (lecture, Haas School of Business, Berkeley, CA, March 23, 2011).

11   Bill Hybels, *Axiom,* (Michigan: Zondervan, 2008), 17.

12   Ibid., 83.

13   Monika Hamori, Jie Cao and Burak Koyuncu. "Why Top Young Managers Are in a Nonstop Job Hunt." *Harvard Business Review,* July-August (2012): 28.

14   Walter Isaacson, *Steve Jobs,* (New York: Simon & Schuster, 2011), 488.

15   Steve Tobak, CBS, "10 Ways to Think Different — Inside Apple's Cult-Like Culture." March 2, 2011. http://www.cbsnews. com/8301-505125_162-28246899/10-ways-to-think-different-- -inside-apples-cult-like-culture.

16   Google, "Ten things we know to be true." http://www.google. com/about/company/philosophy/.

17   Isaacson, Walter. *Steve Jobs.* (New York: Simon & Schuster, 2011), 571.

Let's Go!

Rick

CPSIA information can be obtained at www.ICGtesting.com
Printed in the USA
BVOW071655030113

309525BV00002B/2/P